Grammar Galaxy

Adventures in Language Arts

Nebula

Melanie Wilson, Ph.D.

Rebecca Mueller, Illustrator

Dedicated to future guardians of Grammar Galaxy and to the glory of God.

Special thanks to my family, friends, beta testers, and to Rebecca Mueller for their invaluable help and support. You made Grammar Galaxy a reality.

GRAMMAR GALAXY: NEBULA
Copyright © 2016 by Fun to Learn Books

ISBN: 978-0-9965703-0-5

Table of Contents

A Note to Teachers

I'm passionate about language arts. I love to read, write, and speak. As a homeschooling mom, I wanted my own children and my friends' children to share my passion. Over the years, I found aspects of many different curricula that clicked with my students. But I never found something that did everything I wanted a complete curriculum for elementary students to do:

- Use the most powerful medium to teach language arts: story
- Give the why of language arts to motivate students
- Teach to mastery rather than drill the same concepts year after year
- Limit seat work and use little-to-no-prep games to teach instead
- Teach skills like reading fluency, handwriting speed, and public speaking

I felt called to create my own fast, easy, and fun curriculum for homeschooling parents and others who want to see students succeed in language arts.

Grammar Galaxy: Nebula is for students who are just beginning to read and write. This curriculum does not take the place of beginning phonics and handwriting instruction. It is also meant to be read to students. The stories and concepts are appropriate for students in first to sixth grade, however, making this a perfect read aloud for families. Be sure to point out the synonyms for vocabulary words that are provided. Following each story, there are questions to ask your student to check for understanding. With your help, the student should complete the corresponding mission in the *Mission Manual* before moving on to the next story. The *Mission Manual* can be purchased at GrammarGalaxyBooks.com.

My hope is that your student will accept the call to be a guardian of Grammar Galaxy.

Melanie Wilson

Unit I: Adventures in Literature

Chapter I

It was Saturday morning. The three English children, Kirk, Luke, and Ellen, sat playing their favorite video game. Their dog, Comet, lay next to them, looking bored.

This was the usual order for a weekend on their planet. Their parents were the King and Queen of English. They wouldn't normally request their presence until lunch time.

Today was different. The king and queen hurried into the game room looking upset. Kirk and Ellen stopped playing immediately and stood to greet their parents.

"What is it, Mother?" Ellen asked.

"Yes, Father, is there a problem?" Kirk asked. Kirk was the oldest and was eager to please.

"There is indeed a problem," the king responded. He seemed more worried than Kirk could ever remember.

"It involves all of you," the queen explained. When she saw that young Luke was still focused on the game, she sighed. "Luke, you must stop playing and listen," she said sternly. Luke glanced up and was convinced his mother was serious. He put his game controller down and stood to join them.

"Children, our planet and all of Grammar Galaxy are being threatened," the king said.

Kirk stood tall and said, "Father, I will do whatever is necessary to protect our planet. You can trust me."

The king put his hand on Kirk's shoulder. "I believe I can, Kirk. But this is a problem you cannot solve alone. You will need your brother and sister to help you."

Kirk looked at his younger sister Ellen and wondered how she could help him fight a real enemy. She wasn't very good at fighting video-game aliens! Ellen seemed to read his mind and putting her hands on her hips, said, "I will also protect our planet, Father."

Both of the elder English children turned to look at Luke. He had a gift for gaming but had a difficult time paying attention to much of anything else. They wondered how they could possibly need his help. "I'll fight too!" Luke proclaimed, pretending to kick and punch aliens. Little Comet barked his approval. The king couldn't help but smile at his children's courage. But they didn't know what was happening. He asked the children to take a seat and ordered the screen to play a commercial.

Kids appeared on the screen who were using gaming devices to fire at alien ships. The game-playing kids laughed and smiled while an announcer spoke. "Our children...the hope of Grammar Galaxy. They can learn the battle skills they will need to defeat aliens in the future, or..."

The screen changed to images of children bored with books. "...we can insist that children waste their time on books," the announcer sneered. "The future belongs to gamers...not readers." The commercial ended with a boy and girl celebrating their destruction of an alien ship. The announcer rapidly concluded, "Paid for by Citizens for a Better Galaxy."

"That was awesome!" Luke exclaimed. "Do you want us to become better gamers so we can save the galaxy?"

"No," his father answered, getting louder. "That's the *opposite* of what we want."

"Children," the queen began. "Grammar Galaxy owes its very existence to books."

"Yes," Luke interrupted. "But games are the future!"

"No," the king said a little too harshly. He calmed himself and said, "Grammar Galaxy will disappear without books. Let me explain." The king stood and commanded the screen to display a graphic of Grammar Galaxy.

"Here is planet English," he said, pointing. "You know that anything that happens around the galaxy affects our citizens. In the same way, anything we do on planet English affects the galaxy."

The three English children nodded. "This ad campaign is telling parents to stop having their children read. It is changing life on our planet and in the galaxy at large." The king began to pace as he went on. "The head librarian of our English libraries requested an emergency meeting with me. She told me that she will not be purchasing any more books because children aren't checking them out.

★ ★ ★ ★ ★ ★ ★ ★ ★ ★

exquisite – *beautiful*

inestimable – *valuable*

tenacity – *determination*

★ ★ ★ ★ ★ ★ ★ ★ ★ ★

"That's just the beginning. Because children aren't reading, words on planet Vocabulary are dying. They aren't being used because they aren't being learned in books. Look!"

The king ordered the screen to switch to a live feed of planet Vocabulary. The words **exquisite**, **inestimable**, and **tenacity** faced the camera, looking pale and weak. "I don't know those words, Father," Luke said sadly.

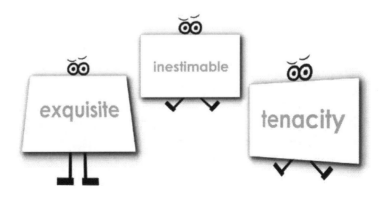

"I'm not surprised, Luke. If you don't start reading, there are many words you will never know. And Vocabulary isn't the only planet in trouble. Show planet Spelling," the king ordered.

The screen showed letters running around in a panic. "What's wrong with them, Father?" Ellen asked.

"They don't know their place anymore. Children aren't reading books, so they aren't learning how words are spelled," her father explained.

"The poor things look exhausted," her mother added.

★ ★ ★ ★ ★ ★ ★ ★ ★ ★

composition – *writing*

★ ★ ★ ★ ★ ★ ★ ★ ★ ★

"The worst news of all is that our largest planet is failing. Go to planet **Composition**," the king said. The screen gave a wide-angle view of the planet and then zoomed in to show Poetry City, deserted.

"Where are all the poems, Father?" Kirk asked.

"The same place as all the stories, papers, and books," his father answered. "They're leaving Grammar Galaxy." He turned back to the screen. "Show Export City." Poems, stories, papers, and books were boarding ships bound for planet Recycling. "You see, when children don't read, they stop writing. They have fewer words to use, they don't know how to spell, and they aren't inspired to write. All these written works will disappear."

"What about the writing on the Internet?" Kirk asked.

"With fewer visitors reading, websites will be shut down. We will lose everything that took years to create," his mother said.

"This is a disaster!" Kirk exclaimed.

"Yes, Kirk, it is. I'm glad you understand," the king answered.

"Why are these advertisements being run if reading is so important to the survival of the galaxy?" Kirk asked.

"Very good question, my son," answered the queen. "We believe this is the work of our enemy."

"Video game makers?" suggested Luke.

"No, dear, though I understand why you think they're the problem. Instead, our galaxy's enemy is..." she explained.

"The Gremlin," the king and queen said together.

"From the beginning of Grammar Galaxy, he has sought to destroy us. He is most likely behind these advertisements," the king said.

"Father, just get him and put him in the dungeon!" Luke jumped up and pretended to slam the Gremlin into a cell.

The king grinned at his youngest son. "The problem is we can't see the Gremlin. But we can see the damage he does—damage we have to try to fix right away."

"Just tell us what to do," Kirk said.

"You have to get the children of planet English reading again."

"How can we do that, Father? We're just children ourselves," Ellen asked.

The king drew his children close. He raised his hands over them and declared, "You are no longer just the royal children of planet English. You are Guardians of Grammar Galaxy. I give you the authority to assign our young people missions that can defeat the Gremlin. With their help, I know you can save the galaxy."

A servant entered the game room carrying a book, which the queen took from him. "You will need this," she said, handing the book to Kirk.

Luke and Ellen were eager to see it, and Ellen was first to read the book's title, *The Guide to Grammar Galaxy*. The children stared at it and wondered what could be written in it that would be of help to them.

"We are always here for you, children. But you must learn to rely on this guidebook if there is any hope for us," the king said, reaching for his wife's hand.

When his parents left the room, Luke broke the silence. "Okay, are you guys up for another game of Super Nova?"

"Luke, this is serious!" Ellen warned.

"I *am* serious. I want to play!"

Kirk ignored his siblings and opened the guidebook to the table of contents—the list of topics that were in the book. "The Importance of Reading" was the first entry, which he read to his brother and sister.

The Importance of Reading
The more you read, the better reader you will become. The better reader you are, the more you will know. The more you know, the more likely you are to get good grades, get a job you love someday, and even get along with others.

The good news is you don't have to read boring books to get all the benefits of reading. Reading books you enjoy will help you increase your vocabulary (the words you know). You will also learn to spell and write well. If you don't read many books now, you can start today and still be a good reader. One of the best ways to find books you like is to go to the library. Reading books that are easy for you is a good place to start. But spend some time trying to read books that are a little more challenging too. Read out loud, listen to audiobooks, and have someone read to you.

"Now what do we do?" Ellen asked when Kirk finished reading from the guidebook.

Kirk looked thoughtful and then certain. "We give kids a mission."

Once they had decided on a mission to solve the crisis, Ellen had an idea. She suggested giving each young person on the planet a mission manual. Luke insisted on getting a manual as well. Mission 1 on the importance of reading was written. It was then delivered to every young person on the planet with high hopes of saving Grammar Galaxy.

What does *composition* mean?

Do you like to read?

What would happen if everyone stopped reading and played video games instead?

Chapter 2

The king was delighted to hear from the head librarian. She was thrilled about the number of library books being checked out. He was also pleased to get encouraging reports from planets Vocabulary, Spelling, and Composition. He and the queen brought Kirk, Luke, and Ellen to the throne room to congratulate them on a mission well done. Comet trotted along behind them, sure he had earned a reward too.

All three children were proud that they had succeeded, but Kirk was quick to give credit to the young people of the planet who had helped them. Ellen was **ecstatic** that the mission manuals were a hit. Luke was happy to have found some *Star Battle* books at the library. He showed them to his mother who suggested he read out loud for them.

★ ★ ★ ★ ★ ★ ★ ★ ★ ★

ecstatic – *thrilled*

fibbing – *lying*

excursion – *trip*

★ ★ ★ ★ ★ ★ ★ ★ ★ ★

Luke gladly agreed. "An enemy drone approached the star ship and the captain told his crew, 'Be ready to—" Luke looked up from the book in surprise. "The next word just disappeared!"

His mother assumed he just didn't know the word and was **fibbing** to cover for it until she took the book from him. She looked up in surprise. "He's right. It's gone!"

"What in the world?" the king exclaimed. He commanded the throne room screen to search for an explanation. Soon a spaceship appeared on the screen. "Zoom in!" the king ordered. As the camera focused on the large windows of the ship, multiple words could be seen on board.

The whole English family looked at one another. They wondered what these words were doing away from the sentences and books they belonged to. "Give me some background on this **excursion**," the king requested, suddenly alarmed.

After some time, the screen gave a report. "Words that have more than one meaning received an invitation to go on a trip to explore their roots. Hundreds of words accepted."

"Can you get me a passenger list?"

"Yes, right away, Your Majesty," the screen answered.

"Father, what's going on?" Kirk asked.

"If I'm right, our young people are going to have great difficulty reading. Words are missing from books. Without knowing which sentences they left, it will be harder to determine what they mean. This has to be the work of the Gremlin! He won't stop trying to discourage kids from reading, because he knows it's how to destroy the galaxy. I'm afraid you children have another mission. I have made you guardians of this galaxy and now only you have the power to stop the Gremlin. You did so well in your last mission. I have to trust that you will manage this one too." He turned to the queen. "Dear, let's leave them to their work and go for a, a..."

"A what?" she asked.

"For the life of me, I can't say it! I know what I mean. I want to calm down by going for a, a..."

"Oh, I know, dear. You want to go for a, a...I can't say it either!"

Each child knew what their father had meant to say, but was stunned that they were also unable to say it.

"It's more serious than I thought," the king admitted. "You children will have to get busy right away." He and the queen left, looking worried.

"What do we do now?" Luke asked, sharing his parents' worry.

Kirk began to pace as his father often did when he needed to think. Then Ellen suddenly left the room. Both boys were surprised by her exit. They understood when she returned with the guidebook. Ellen opened the book to the table of contents. She drew her finger down the page and said, "I'm not even sure what I'm looking for."

"Father said that we don't know the meanings of these words when they're away from their sentences. Does that help?" Kirk offered.

"I think it might. Wait a minute..." Ellen continued scanning through the pages and stopped, reading silently. "That's it!" she said and began reading to the boys.

Determining Meaning from Context

Good readers pay attention to the **context**. Context is the pictures and other words surrounding an unknown word. Context is especially important for **homographs**. Homographs are words that are spelled the same but have different meanings. The sentence starting, "I gave my dog a ___" is more likely to end with the words *bath or treat* than the word *kangaroo*. If there is a picture of a bathtub, *bath* is the most likely choice. We know this from the context. The homograph *batter* has two different meanings depending on which sentence it is in. For example: The *batter* tasted delicious when she added the sugar. vs. The *batter* would be out if he got one more strike. The other words in the sentences give us clues to the correct meaning of the homographs.

"Okay, this makes sense," Ellen said. "Luke, open your book again and let's look at words and any pictures around the missing word. They're our clues to this mystery." Luke was quick to cooperate and opened the book to where he left off. The two of them studied the picture of a captain and a crew member seated at the control panel of a spaceship. The crew member had his finger over a big red button.

He read again, "An enemy drone approached the star ship and the captain told his crew, 'Be ready to...'"

"Keep reading," Ellen urged.

"'Be ready to...on my command!'" Luke looked up. "I think I know what the word is!" Kirk and Ellen nodded in agreement. "It's one of those humma, hummag—"

"Homographs," Ellen finished for him. "Yes. It has more than one meaning."

Kirk was frustrated. "We know this missing word, but how are we going to get all the other homographs back where they belong?"

While they were discussing ideas, the screen announced that it had the requested passenger list. That's when Kirk remembered something he had read. "'The best evidence is first-hand evidence.' That's what Sherlock Holmes said."

"Who's Sherlock Holmes?" Luke asked.

"He's a detective in a series of mystery books."

"Okay. So what is first-hand evidence?"

"It's evidence we see for ourselves. Screen," Kirk commanded, "prepare our shuttle for a trip to planet Sentence."

Aboard the shuttle, Kirk explained that Sherlock wanted to see the scene of a crime to help solve it.

"But this isn't really a crime," Luke argued.

"No, but it's a mystery. To solve it, we need to see the sentences whose words are missing and look for clues."

The trip was uneventful, except for a few times when they couldn't say the word they were thinking. The three guardians didn't have to go far from the shuttle to find upset sentences. Kirk let them all know they were there to help. Ellen read one troubled sentence out loud.

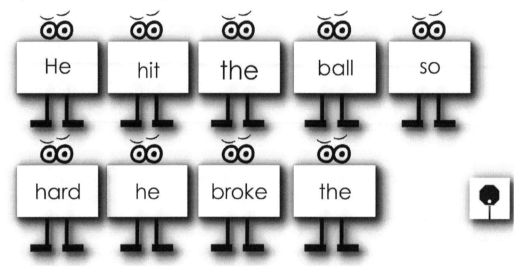

Kirk was excited. "It's elementary, my dear Watson!"

"What are you talking about, Kirk?" Ellen asked, wondering if Kirk had a case of space sickness.

"Sherlock Holmes's assistant was Dr. Watson. Sherlock liked to say that the process of solving mysteries was elementary, or simple. Some of these words are clues to identifying the missing word. They're like eye-witnesses," Kirk explained.

Some of the words looked alarmed until Kirk told them that they weren't suspects—just witnesses.

"What's a suspect?" Luke asked.

"Someone you think could have committed a crime," Ellen answered.

"Oh. No wonder these guys seemed so nervous!" Luke said.

"Some of these words aren't good clues. They go with many words," Kirk continued.

"Like *the*?" Luke suggested.

"Exactly," Kirk said.

Kirk discussed the sentence with Luke and Ellen. They asked the following words to step forward: *hit, ball,* and *broke.* The three paced back and forth in front of the words, thinking. They stopped in front of the word *hit.*

"*Hit* is a clue, but not a very good one. You can hit lots of things," Kirk said.

"Yes," Ellen said stepping to the next word, "but the sentence says whatever it is hit the ball."

"Right," Luke responded, walking to the last word, "and then it broke. There's only one word that makes sense in this sentence."

Kirk and Ellen looked at one another knowingly. They found the suspected missing word on the homograph passenger list.

"We still have to get this missing word home. And look at all these sad sentences! How will we ever solve all these mysteries ourselves?" Ellen asked.

"We won't, Ellen, but we don't have to. We have our fellow guardians, remember? And I have a plan to get the homographs home." Kirk opened his communicator and ordered, "Get me Grammar Patrol." When the captain answered, Kirk asked him to stop the homographs' ship. The officers were to ask the words for their papers, which they wouldn't have. They could then order the words to return to their planets at once.

The three of them then decided on the details of the mission, "Reading from Context." They added it to their fellow guardians' manuals. They then worked together to solve more sentence mysteries, knowing that help was on the way.

What does *excursion* mean?

What did the king want to take with the queen so he could calm down?

What word was missing from Luke's book?
"Be ready to _____ on my command!"

Chapter 3

The king and queen were once again pleased with their children's work. They planned a special celebration in their honor. Everyone was seated in the dining room, including Comet, who wore a bib to protect his white fur from what was sure to be a messy meal.

While they were waiting to be served, the king's servant presented a scroll to Kirk. Kirk read several paragraphs on the scroll out loud, smiling.

"What do you think of my plan, Kirk?" the king asked. Kirk stared at his father, still smiling, but did not answer. "Kirk? Do you have an opinion?" he repeated.

Kirk seemed confused. "What plan, Father?"

"The plan you just read about!" his father responded, becoming impatient. When Kirk shrugged, the king said, "Luke, Ellen, what do you think?"

"Of what?" the two answered.

"The plan!" the king said, nearly shouting.

"Ohhhhh, the plan," Ellen replied sweetly. "Well..."

"Yes?" the king leaned in to hear his daughter's opinion.

"I don't actually know what you mean by the plan," she was embarrassed to admit.

"What is going on here?" the king roared.

"Dear, why don't you just tell us the plan. Then we'll give you our opinion," the queen said, trying to calm her husband.

"Kirk just read the plan!" The king's face reddened in frustration until he realized what was happening. "Great Grammar! You didn't understand anything that was read, did you?" Each of them agreed that they had not. "This is a **dilemma**."

★ ★ ★ ★ ★ ★ ★ ★ ★ ★

dilemma – *problem*

★ ★ ★ ★ ★ ★ ★ ★ ★ ★

There was an uncomfortable silence until Luke interjected. "I have an idea. Let's eat and worry about it later."

Even the king couldn't help but laugh and agreed that they could talk about it over dinner.

Later, the king asked Luke to get one of his books to read for them. Comet didn't follow him, choosing to stay under the table where he could allow his big meal to digest.

Luke opened his book and began, "The guh...rrr...eee...nnn...ay...lll... eee...uhh."

"What on English? Why are you reading that way?" cried the queen.

Tears began to well up in Luke's eyes. "I don't know! I've been reading a lot. I promise!"

"Luke, I believe you. It's not your fault. Something else is going on here," the king explained. "Ellen, do you have any guesses as to what it is?"

Ellen looked up from her communicator that she had been using on her lap. "Any guesses as to *what*?"

"Ellen!" her mother corrected her. "Haven't you been listening?"

"Sure. Yes—I just—"

"You haven't," the king interrupted. "Dear, I need to take a walk after that big meal and this time I'm happy I can say the word. But I'm not happy that our children have yet another problem to solve. Comet, come! You can use the exercise too."

The three children wore sorry expressions as they watched their parents and dog leave. "We really blew it," Kirk admitted. His brother

15

and sister nodded sadly. "I just don't understand why I couldn't remember anything I'd read."

"I don't understand why I was having such a hard time reading, period," Luke agreed.

Ellen looked guilty. "I know what my problem was, but you two weren't looking at your communicators." She thought for a moment. "We need the guidebook."

The boys waited for Ellen to get the book from the library and looked through the table of contents with her when she returned. They finally found an entry about their problem.

Reading Comprehension

Reading comprehension is the ability to understand what is read. Comprehension can be affected when:
   * There is a problem with vision or hearing (if someone is being read to)
   * Words are read too slowly to be understood, possibly because of poor phonics skills
   * The reader is distracted and can't focus on the reading
   * Memory skills aren't being used to remember what is read

Every effort should be made to improve reading comprehension. Achievement in every subject, including math, is related to it. Students with vision, hearing, or reading problems should get professional help. Students should practice to improve phonics and word recognition skills. Distractions like TV and digital devices should be eliminated during reading. Reading memory skills should also be developed by answering questions about the text.

"I could see what I was reading just fine and I haven't noticed that any of us has trouble hearing," Kirk said.

"I was reading too slowly, but I thought I knew my phonics pretty well," Luke said, still looking upset.

"Luke, you have been reading well. This is so confusing. Wait! You know what we haven't done yet? We haven't had Screen help us." Ellen commanded the dining room screen to search for problems on planet Spelling. During the search, Luke asked her why she was focusing on Spelling. "Because Phonics City is there. I just have a feeling we'll find the cause of the problem there."

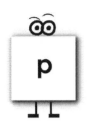

All three guardians watched as the screen zoomed in to show Phonics City. Thousands of **phonemes** were lined up behind a sign that read KARAOKE CONTEST ENTRY HERE. Kirk touched the screen at the head of the line to enlarge the view. A *p* phoneme was up on the stage. The *p* could be heard singing its sound over and over while the music blared. After the music stopped, one judge started asking the phoneme questions about its career.

The three children looked at one another, **astounded** by what they were seeing. The phoneme kept repeating its sound in answer to questions. After a few more minutes, the last judge said, "I think we agree. We want to hear more from you! Go to the end of the line and show us what else you've got." The other two judges clapped and said, "Yes, yes!" The phoneme started walking off the stage.

★ ★ ★ ★ ★ ★ ★ ★ ★ ★

phonemes – *units of sound*

astounded – *shocked*

★ ★ ★ ★ ★ ★ ★ ★ ★ ★

"OK, that's just weird," Luke said.

"You've got that right," Ellen agreed. "But it's not good for another reason."

"What do you mean?" Kirk asked.

"This is why Luke was taking so long to sound out his phonemes when he was reading. The phonemes are trying to be stars on their own instead of working together to make words. Besides that, they're having to wait so long to even make a sound," Ellen explained.

"I think you're right. We need to get to planet Spelling fast," Kirk said. "We don't have time for the shuttle; we'll use the space porter." Kirk hurried his two siblings to the porter, ignoring Luke's questions on the way.

When the group appeared at Phonics City, the karaoke line was even longer than it had looked on screen. They walked quickly to the front of the line where a muscular man tried to block their way. "Phonemes only!" he barked.

"Sir, I am Prince Kirk. Let us pass," Kirk requested calmly.

The security guard let him go, muttering that he wasn't getting paid enough to argue. The trio marched up to the judges' table. One of them, an attractive young lady, seemed excited to see them. "Oh! Are you here to sing? Great!"

"No, we're here to stop the competition," Ellen said as confidently as she could.

"Oh good," another young woman at the judges' table groaned. "This couldn't be any more boring."

"Wait, do we still get our checks?" the third young judge asked. Kirk questioned the three of them. He learned that they had been invited to judge a karaoke competition for pay. They had no idea that only phonemes would participate. When Kirk assured the judge that he would still be paid and took his information, he left quickly. "Later!" he called back to the other judges.

The children got contact information from the remaining judges and the security guard. Then they faced an angry crowd of phonemes. The phonemes began making their sounds to express disapproval. Kirk grabbed a microphone and explained that they all had talent. "But," he continued, "you really shine when you're in a group. Get together and you'll make beautiful music. We'll bring the competition back when you've had plenty of time to work together."

The phonemes quickly took to the idea and began forming groups. The three English children requested a return trip via the space porter and were home in moments.

Kirk, Luke, and Ellen formed a group of their own and began writing a mission called "Reading Comprehension." They hoped it would solve the crisis.

What is reading comprehension?

Why didn't Ellen know what Kirk read on the scroll at dinner?

What was happening in Phonics City that hurt reading comprehension?

Chapter 4

Kirk, Luke, and Ellen were spending time in the observatory before bed. The three had brought their bowls of ice cream with them to enjoy the view of the stars. When they finished their dessert, Ellen cuddled with Comet in a comfy chair. The boys walked around trying to identify constellations and planets in their galaxy.

The moon was full and bright, casting a glow into the room. It was so beautiful that Luke had to stop his searching to sit and admire it. Something so strange caught his eye that he thought he must have been dreaming. He rubbed his eyes and pinched himself to make sure he was awake.

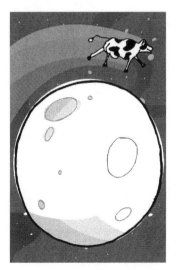

"Guys," he said. "I think I just saw a cow jump over the moon."

Kirk and Ellen erupted in laughter. "Good one," Ellen said, congratulating Luke on his humor.

"No, I'm serious."

Kirk looked at Luke like he wasn't thinking straight. "You need to go to bed, Luke."

Luke protested until all three of them saw an ice cream bowl and spoon get up from the table, jump down to the floor, and run out of the room. Comet barked and gave chase but quickly stopped and whined fearfully.

"And the dish ran away with the spoon..." Ellen said.

"What was in that ice cream?" Kirk asked, holding his stomach.

The threesome left the observatory in a hurry, with Comet following close behind. All three of them spoke at once when they arrived at the door of their parents' bedchamber. "Children, what is it? One at a time," the queen said, trying to calm them.

Kirk explained what they had seen. The queen smiled and said, "You're all just tired. I see things all the time when I'm sleepy."

"Yes, you do," the king agreed, yawning.

"Mother, I thought that was it too, but how could we all have seen the same thing?" Luke asked.

Before she could answer, a young woman in a jeweled ball gown rushed past them, dropping a glass slipper. She continued running awkwardly in one shoe toward the staircase.

"Cinderella?" Ellen said in awe. "Did you see her too?"

"Yes," the queen answered, seeming faint.

"Mother, did you also have the ice cream?" Ellen asked.

"No, no ice cream. But I'm not feeling well." Ellen helped her mother over to the bed so she could lie down.

The king seemed annoyed that his bedtime had been disturbed. "Listen, we're all tired and all of this nonsense will be cleared up with a good night's sleep. Off to bed!" he ordered.

He went to close the door when a young man dressed in **regal** clothing came running up and stooped to pick up the slipper. He cradled the shoe in his hands and walked sadly toward the stairs. "I must find her," he said, unaware that the English family was staring at him.

★ ★ ★ ★ ★ ★ ★ ★ ★ ★

regal – *royal*

mystified – *confused*

fitfully – *poorly*

★ ★ ★ ★ ★ ★ ★ ★ ★ ★

Everyone was **mystified** by what they'd seen and looked to the king for guidance. "Okay! Something is going on," he admitted. "But we can't do anything about it tonight. Let's go to bed and meet in the morning to investigate."

The children reluctantly went to their rooms, feeling very uneasy. Each slept **fitfully**, dreaming of strange events, wondering if they were really happening.

In the morning, Kirk, Luke, and Ellen found the king and queen in the dining room. Their parents looked just as exhausted as they felt. The king encouraged everyone to eat their breakfast, but he only picked at his own eggs. Even Comet seemed to have lost his appetite.

All were relieved when the king announced that he was going to get to the bottom of the mystery. "Screen, status update," he commanded. Soon live video appeared from their planet. A wolf stood on two legs outside a little house made of straw.

Faintly, a voice could be heard from within the house saying, "I will not let you in. Not by the hair of my chinny chin chin."

The wolf answered, "Then I'll huff and I'll puff and I'll blow your house in!"

"I think he means it!" Luke cried.

"That's not what I'm worried about," the king said. "Children, you have another mission. You will need to act quickly, or the safety of everyone on planet English is in danger!" He took the queen's hand. "Dear, come with me. Usually the princess is at most risk, but I'm not going to take any chances." The two of them left, carrying a weary Comet with them.

Kirk was the first to remember the need for the guidebook this time. He led his siblings to the castle library where it was kept. "What are we looking for?" Kirk asked them as he opened the book.

"Well, fairy tales and nursery rhymes are coming to life," Ellen replied. "Is there anything about that in the table of contents?"

Kirk searched, but couldn't find anything. "Too bad there isn't anything listed for 'strange.'"

"Yes, this has been really strange alright. Stranger than...wait! Have you heard the saying, 'Truth is stranger than fiction'? Fiction is the category for fairy tales and nursery rhymes. See if there is anything on fiction," Ellen said.

Soon Kirk found an entry.

Fiction vs. Nonfiction

Imaginary stories, poems, and books are **fiction**. Fictional works aren't real. Fiction = fairy tale is an easy way to remember this. Some examples are books about super heroes, stories about the future, and cartoons.

Nonfiction works are true stories or information. Nonfiction books are more likely to have a table of contents, maps, or graphs. Some examples are biographies, science books, and encyclopedias.

Some books have characteristics of both fiction and nonfiction. For example, a novel (a longer fiction book) may be about a made-up character living during events that really happened. The library lists every book as fiction or nonfiction.

Kirk seemed to have identified a clue from the guidebook and wasted no time calling on Screen to help. "Screen, search the planetary library system for Grimm's Fairy Tales."

"What are Grimm's Fairy Tales?" Luke asked while they waited.

"They are a collection of folk tales—stories passed down by telling and retelling. They were put into a book by two brothers named Grimm. The brothers lived on planet German a long time ago. The book was so popular that it is in the libraries of more than 70 planets like ours," Kirk explained.

Soon the listing for *Grimm's Fairy Tales* appeared on the screen. "Scroll down," Kirk requested. He gasped at what he read and then asked Screen to search for *Mother Goose Nursery Rhymes*. He reacted the same way to what he saw.

"Kirk, what is it?" Ellen asked.

"If I'm right, a boy named Jack is going to be jumping over a candlestick. Fiction books have been listed as nonfiction and they're coming to life!"

"Cool!" Luke exclaimed, looking excited until he saw his older brother's reaction.

"Not cool, Luke. Every monster and evil being will eventually come to life and destroy our planet. We have to do something."

"How did this happen?" Ellen asked and then answered her own question. "The Gremlin."

"Yes. He must have somehow accessed the library catalog and classified all books as nonfiction."

"Why haven't we heard from the head librarian?" Ellen asked.

Kirk asked the screen to show the main library. A huge spider hung down over the circulation desk. A giant shoe house had upended tables and chairs. An old woman was chasing children through the library. The three could hear the woman saying, "I don't know what to do!"

"Uh, I think the head librarian is gone," Kirk announced.

"I sure wouldn't stay!" Luke cried.

"Now what?" Ellen asked, sounding as stressed as the old woman. "Can you change the book category back to fiction?"

"Yes, but I'd have to do it for every fiction book. It would take forever!" Kirk groaned.

"Not if we ask our fellow guardians to help," Luke said calmly.

Luke's older siblings looked at him and smiled, realizing he was right. Kirk asked Screen to change *Grimm's Fairy Tales* and *Mother*

Goose Nursery Rhymes back to fiction. Then the three began working on a mission to be added to the guardians' manuals called "Identifying Fiction and Nonfiction."

What does *mystified* mean?

What did the guidebook say fiction was equal (=) to?

What fairy tale came to life outside the king and queen's bedchamber?

Chapter 5

It took a few weeks for English citizens to stop expecting fictional characters to come to life. Comet had remained in hiding every day. The head librarian was so traumatized by the giant spider that she asked for a leave of absence. The king understood and gave her permission to take time off.

The three guardians were also hopeful that they could have a break. They decided to spend an afternoon at the main library branch finding new books to read.

Ellen was excited to get another book by Laura Ingalls Wilder. She had loved *Little House on the Prairie* so she checked out the first book in the series, *Little House in the Big Woods*. Kirk chose Tolkien's *Return of the King*. Luke thought *Click, Clack, Moo: Cows That Type* looked funny. The three picked out a few nonfiction books and a couple of movies and headed to the checkout counter.

The main library allowed patrons to check out materials themselves. Normally, this worked well. But this time, the children couldn't get the green light for a successful checkout. Finally, Kirk tried to get the attention of the library assistant.

"Excuse me, Miss? We can't seem to get these books checked out. Can you help?"

The young woman seemed distracted by the computer but came over to explain that the system was down. She scanned the kids' cards and then their books to deactivate the alarm. "Of course, you are free to keep the books as long as you like. But the system says they are due back in two weeks," she told them.

"There will be no problem returning them. Thank you so much," Kirk said **graciously**.

★ ★ ★ ★ ★ ★ ★ ★ ★ ★

graciously – *politely*

sequel – *part two*

★ ★ ★ ★ ★ ★ ★ ★ ★ ★

The three royals walked home with their finds, enjoying the fresh air and the exercise. After a late afternoon snack, each went to a favorite reading spot and started a book.

Ellen had grown to love little Laura and wanted to read about her life before the prairie. Laura was the same Laura, but as she read, Ellen kept looking at the cover to make sure she had gotten the right book. In this book, Laura lived in Fangorn Forest. She typed letters to ask a farmer for warm blankets. Ellen thought it was strange and a rare case when the **sequel** was better than the first book.

At dinner, the three siblings told their parents what titles they had chosen. When asked what they thought of them so far, no one spoke.

"Children, what's wrong? Don't you like your books?" the queen asked.

Luke finally answered. "I thought it was going to be funny. So far it's just weird. Cows are preparing to fight a huge battle to overcome evil in the woods of Wisconsin."

The three children realized what was wrong at the same time and talked over one another until the king interrupted and asked what was going on.

"Our books seem to have gotten mixed up," Ellen explained.

"Well, just exchange them, and then we can have dessert," the king said, proud of his simple solution.

"I wish it were that easy, Father," Ellen answered. "When I say mixed up, I mean parts of our books have gotten mixed up."

"Do you mean someone has torn out pages of your books and pasted them into others? I will severely punish him!" the king threatened.

"Father, it's worse than that. The pages haven't been mixed up. The words have been," Kirk said.

The king groaned and then asked that dessert be served, saying it would help them all think more clearly. When they finished, he said, "Start from the beginning. You got the books from the main library?"

"Yes, Father," Ellen said. "Everything seemed normal, except we had trouble checking out the books. The assistant librarian said the system was down."

"I wasn't made aware of this. Our library system is top-notch. I know the Gremlin got into it and caused the fiction fiasco. But I'm sure we've taken steps to prevent that in the future," the king said confidently.

Kirk didn't share his father's confidence. "Father, did the head librarian improve our library system's security before she left?"

"I...don't know," he admitted.

"Then the Gremlin may have attacked the library system again."

"Maybe not!" Luke chimed in. "The library assistant was playing Sonic Boom when we were checking out."

"How do you know that? Are you tattling again?" Ellen asked.

"Let's just say I've played it enough to know the sounds. Mother says it's not tattling if someone is in trouble. We're in trouble! Sonic Boom is an Internet download and it includes spyware that can mess up your computer. Right, Kirk?"

"Right. It took me forever to get Luke's computer cleaned up and I'm pretty good at it, if I do say so myself. The library assistant could have **corrupted** the files."

★ ★ ★ ★ ★ ★ ★ ★ ★ ★

corrupted – *damaged*

★ ★ ★ ★ ★ ★ ★ ★ ★ ★

"In English please, son," the queen asked.

"Mother, I think the books are messed up because the assistant librarian used a bad computer program."

"Oh dear!" she cried.

"Don't worry, my queen. Our children are wonderful guardians. They will solve this problem and get our books back in order. Right, children?" the king asked.

The children nodded but looked defeated when their parents left to take Comet for a walk in the garden.

"This is a nightmare!" Ellen wailed.

"No, it was a nightmare when the fiction books were labeled nonfiction. This is just a...mess," Kirk said. He suggested looking up their books' summaries in the library system and the younger two agreed it was a good idea. Just as they suspected, the book descriptions were all wrong.

The children discussed solutions when Luke interjected, "We haven't checked the guidebook!" His older siblings thanked him for the reminder and the three of them proceeded to the castle library.

They didn't expect to find an entry on mixed-up books, so weren't sure where to start. When they found an article on story elements, Kirk remembered that elements are basic parts. If the information was on the parts of a story, he hoped it would be helpful to them.

Story Elements

The elements, or main parts, of a story include the setting, characters, and plot.

The **setting** of a story is *when* the events occur — a year, a season, or time of day. The setting is also *where* the story happens. It may include the part of the world, a building, or specific room. Finally, the setting can include the mood. Mood means the feeling. Cobwebs, happy music, and cheers can all help to create the *mood* and setting for a story. You can remember the word *setting* by thinking of setting the table. How you set the table (fancy dishes or paper plates, for example) can tell you what kind of people will be there. It will also tell you if it is a party or regular meal. The setting of a story tells you what to expect.

Characters of a story are who the story is about. Characters are usually people, but they can also be animals and objects that act like people. Characters can be good or evil or anything between. *Character* is also the word we use to describe how good someone is, so that may help you to remember the term.

The **plot** of a story is what happens. The two main parts of a plot are the *problem* and the *solution*. In the story, "The Little Red Hen," the problem is that the hen needs help making bread, but the other animals won't help her. The solution is she makes it with her chicks and doesn't share the bread with the other animals when it's done. The word *plot* can also mean plan. In the story of the three little pigs, the wolf had a plot to eat the pigs. The plot is like the plan of the story.

"Are you thinking what I'm thinking?" Ellen asked.

"If you're thinking what a great game Sonic Boom is, then yes," Luke joked.

"No, be serious, Luke. I'm thinking that the setting, characters, and plots of books have gotten mixed up."

"That's what I was thinking, Ellen," Kirk sighed. "I'm just overwhelmed thinking about fixing it."

Ellen reminded Kirk that they had help. Luke suddenly seemed encouraged. "This is like our very own plot! We just need to get to the solution." His older brother and sister agreed and started working with Screen. Soon they included all the details about the mixed-up books in a mission called "Story Elements."

What does *corrupted* mean?

What is the setting of a story?

Who are the characters in this book?

Chapter 6

"It's here! It's here!" the king shouted with excitement. The king was not one to move quickly, but he was practically running.

"What's here, dear?" the queen asked.

The king took a moment to catch his breath. "The biography!" he cried, holding it up **triumphantly**.

"Oh my, no wonder you're excited. I can't wait to read it!"

"Well, you'll have to wait, because I'm going to read it first," the king teased her.

The king's biographer had been **shadowing** him for nearly a year. The result was the large book the king was holding. The children joined their parents when they heard their father's excitement. They passed the book around. Everyone agreed that the cover photo was an excellent choice.

★ ★ ★ ★ ★ ★ ★ ★ ★ ★

triumphantly – *victoriously*

shadowing – *following*

elated – *thrilled*

★ ★ ★ ★ ★ ★ ★ ★ ★ ★

"Now if you'll excuse me," the king said. "I will be in my study reading. Dear, I will take my dinner in there if you don't mind."

At breakfast the following morning, the king's eyes were blood-shot, but he was **elated**. "I loved it!" he exclaimed. The author did a magnificent job of telling my life story and telling the truth. I'm relieved. You never know if a writer will outright lie to sell more books. And I have an announcement to make." As he said this, he tapped his glass of juice with his spoon. It immediately shattered.

"Oh my word!" the queen cried.

The king began grumbling about the quality of the glass. The kitchen staff began scurrying to clean up the mess and the king quickly calmed down.

"As I was saying, I have an announcement. We are going to go on a book tour together. What do you think of hitting the road with me?"

he asked, smacking the table for emphasis. The other end of the table came off the floor, sending all the tableware sliding in the king's direction. The queen screamed. The children gasped.

Once again, the kitchen staff rushed to tidy the table before the king could lose his temper. The king seemed puzzled. "I guess I don't know my own strength!"

After everything was back in order, the family discussed the book tour. Later that evening, the king suggested that they play a trivia game. The children were surprised by his suggestion as he didn't like trivia and wasn't very good at it.

This time, however, the king seemed to have all the answers. After an answer he was especially proud of, he high-fived Kirk. Kirk collapsed in pain. The king looked puzzled as he stared at his hand. "So sorry, Kirk," he apologized.

"It's okay, Father. I'm fine," Kirk said, but it was clear that he wasn't.

At breakfast the next morning, the king had another announcement. But this time, he was careful not to pound on the table. "I have decided to buy a copy of my biography for everyone on the planet." He couldn't wait to hear what his family thought.

Kirk and the queen gasped. Ellen clapped happily and Luke seemed confused.

"But dear," the queen questioned. "Do you have any idea how much that will cost?"

"Money is no object when it comes to our citizens. I'm a generous king, after all," the king boasted.

After breakfast, Kirk pulled Ellen aside and discussed their father's strange behavior. Kirk used his communicator to get a status report on the galaxy. He saw nothing that would explain his father's behavior. "Now what do we do?" he asked.

"Have you read the biography yet?"

"No, have you?"

"No."

The two had the same idea and ran to their father's study to get the book. After they told Luke what was going on, the three decided to take the book to the main library branch.

Once in the library, the three of them skimmed the book.

30

"Wow! This guy really thinks a lot of Father!" Luke exclaimed.

Ellen hushed him. "I know," she whispered. "But how does this explain Father's strange behavior?" Ellen asked.

"Do we need the guidebook?" Luke asked.

"I thought of that too, but what would we look up? Strange behavior?" Kirk answered.

Ellen sat watching the head librarian, who had returned to her position. "What about her?" she asked.

"She's not a guardian," Kirk replied.

"No, but she may know if there's something wrong with this book that we're missing," Ellen responded.

The three English children made their way to the circulation desk, book in hand. "Excuse us," they said. "Can we get your help?"

"Any time I can be of service to the English children is an honor," the librarian said.

"We have a question about this book," Ellen said, handing her the biography.

"Oh! The king's biography! We don't have a copy yet. I can't wait to read it!" she squealed a little too loudly.

"Well, unfortunately, we can't let you keep this copy, but could you skim through it and tell us what you think? We'll wait," Kirk asked.

"Oh my, I'm sure I can't do the book justice with just a skim."

"We don't need you to review it. It's just that, we're wondering if there's anything unusual about this biography. Could you tell us if you see anything?" Ellen pleaded.

"Well, yes, I should be able to do that. But I can't tell you if there are any grammar errors."

The children assured her that they weren't looking for those kinds of details. Then they let her get to reading. While they waited, they looked for more books to check out for themselves.

After some time had passed, the librarian motioned for the children to return to the circulation desk. "Are you sure you want me to give you my opinion? I don't want to be disrespectful in any way," she said.

The three reassured her until she agreed to tell them what she thought.

"Well, it's an interesting book. I was enjoying reading the parts I was able to read. But—"

"But what?" Kirk asked.

"It's unusual for a biography."

31

"In what way?" Kirk quizzed her.

"It doesn't seem very, oh, how can I put this—realistic?" she said, waiting for a negative response.

"Can you explain more what you mean?" Kirk said.

"The book describes the king almost as if he's...super human! I mean, he's a genius, and incredibly strong, and so generous. And that was just in the first few chapters!"

"Most biographies are negative then?" Kirk asked.

"Some biographies are very positive, but this one seems more like a tall tale!" she giggled, then seemed embarrassed. "I'm sorry, I didn't mean—."

"No, it's okay," Ellen reassured her. "That actually helps us."

The three thanked the librarian and returned the book to the king's study. They then used the guidebook to learn more about tall tales.

Tall Tales

Tall tales are stories presented as truth or nonfiction but are too exaggerated or unbelievable to be true. Tall tales are also called fish stories because fishermen sometimes brag about the size of the fish they "almost caught." They are also called legends or folk tales.

Books about Paul Bunyan are tall tales that are written like biographies, even though Paul is probably a made-up character. He was said to be a lightning-fast, giant lumberjack with an enormous blue ox as a sidekick.

Many tall tales are written for children and include the words "tall tale" in the title to set them apart from nonfiction.

"Uh-oh," Luke said. "Father's biography is a tall tale, but it's supposed to be nonfiction and—"

"It's becoming true!" Kirk and Ellen said together.

"So what do we do?" Luke asked.

"I have no idea," Kirk said, looking discouraged.

"Let's talk to the librarian again," Ellen suggested.

Kirk asked Screen to make the connection and the three of them shared the problems they were having with their father. Then they asked if she had any ideas.

"We would need to get the book classified as fiction rather than a biography," she explained.

"How do we do that?" Kirk asked.

"It isn't a small matter. It's already entered into the system as nonfiction. Unless we know how much of the book is exaggerated or unbelievable, we can't change the category."

"It will take us forever to figure that out and by then, Father will have given away the family fortune!" Luke cried.

"What if we get the guardians to help us?" Ellen asked.

"That's it!" Kirk said, congratulating his sister.

The siblings returned home and used their father's book to send out a mission entitled "Tall Tales."

What changes did the king's family see in him?

What was wrong with the king's biography?

What is a tall tale?

Chapter 7

"Luke, what are you learning in school?" the king asked as the family waited for dinner to be served.

"We are learning about poetry. We have to memorize a poem. I like this one by Joyce Kilmer. 'I think that I shall never see, a poem as lovely as an apple,'" Luke recited with great feeling.

The queen giggled. "Dear, I don't think that's how it goes."

"Yes, it does!" Luke said **indignantly**.

"Well, you had most of it right. Go and get the book and you'll see," the queen said sweetly.

Luke marched to his room to retrieve the book and **sullenly** handed it to his mother when he returned. "Here!"

★ ★ ★ ★ ★ ★ ★ ★ ★ ★

indignantly – *angrily*

sullenly – *pouting*

★ ★ ★ ★ ★ ★ ★ ★ ★ ★

"You aren't being respectful to your mother," the king corrected. Luke quickly apologized.

The queen looked for the poem "Trees" in the table of contents and paged through the book until she found it. "Ah, yes, here we are. One of my favorites. I think that I shall never see, a poem as lovely as an apple." The queen was **aghast** at what she'd read, while Luke seemed pleased to be proven right. "'A poem as lovely as an apple'? That's not how it goes."

★ ★ ★ ★ ★ ★ ★ ★ ★ ★

aghast – *shocked*

★ ★ ★ ★ ★ ★ ★ ★ ★ ★

"How does it go, Mother?" Ellen asked.

"I think that I shall never see, a poem as lovely as...as...dear me! I want to say it, but I can't!"

"Not this again," Kirk moaned.

"Something is wrong with this poem!" the queen held her head in her hands and then got up abruptly. Excuse me, please, but I am going to call it a night."

The king nodded his approval. "You've had a long day, dear. I'm sure that's all it is."

The king gave the children permission to leave the table. Then he suggested they play chess before bedtime. Kirk and Ellen were well-matched opponents. But the king always beat Luke, even when he wasn't trying. The four of them moved to the library where the two royal chess sets were kept.

Luke couldn't believe how well he was playing and when he finally called, "Checkmate!" he couldn't keep himself from celebrating at his father's expense. "I'm number one; can't be number two. I just called a checkmate on...the king!"

"That's not right, Luke," his father corrected.

"I know, Father. I shouldn't have made fun. Forgive me."

"You're right that you shouldn't have made fun, but there is another thing wrong with what you said. I just can't put my finger on it. But you did well," the king congratulated him. Luke beamed with pride.

When their father said good-night, the three young guardians headed to their bedrooms too. Luke took a quick bath, changed into his pajamas, and brushed his teeth. Then he pulled out a favorite book that he had memorized because he'd read it so often: *Green Eggs and Ham* by Dr. Seuss. He started to read:

Do you like green eggs and ham?
I do not like them, Samuel.
I do not like green eggs and pork!

"What on English?" he cried. "That's not how it goes!" He picked up another of his favorite Seuss books, *The Cat in the Hat*, and read:

Then our mother came in
And she said to us two,
"Did you have any fun?
Tell me. What did you play?"

"Again!" he said, frustrated. He knew something was seriously wrong. He decided to talk to Kirk and Ellen about it.

Ellen wasn't too happy when Luke appeared at her door waving a book around in dramatic fashion. Luke insisted on reading from *Green Eggs and Ham*. When Ellen agreed that the book no longer read correctly, she also agreed they needed to tell Kirk. Kirk wondered whether there was a connection between their mother's poem problem and the Dr. Seuss books.

Ellen left Kirk talking to himself and came back with the guidebook. "I think we need to look for information on poetry to solve this mystery," she said.

Poetry

Poetry is a form of writing made up of verses that may not be complete sentences. Words in poems are used to create pictures and emotions in the reader. Poetry can also be used to tell stories. Poems often rely on rhythm and often on rhyme. Rhythm is a pattern of stressed (emphasized) and unstressed syllables. Poems that rhyme have verses that end with the same sounds. For example, words like man/can and fly/high rhyme, and could be used at the ends of verses in a rhyming poem.

Luke looked thoughtful and opened *Green Eggs and Ham* and read again:

Do you like green eggs and ham?

I do not like them, Samuel.
I do not like green eggs and pork!

"Ham, Samuel, and pork don't rhyme, do they? They don't end in the same sound and I think they're supposed to," Luke said.

"Yes!" Kirk said, getting excited. "What if we can't use rhyming words and that's what's caused all the problems tonight?"

"Let me see," Ellen replied. "House, rat. Door, wall. Ack! I can't rhyme. I think we've discovered the problem. But how do we fix it?"

"We've discovered the problem, but we don't know why we can't rhyme. Let's head back to the library and do some research," Kirk said. The three siblings hurried to the library, trying to be quiet so as not to awaken their parents.

Once there, Kirk asked Screen to search for any news having to do with rhyming words. It wasn't long before the three were watching a commercial discovered in the search. Sad music played while a word looked out over a lake at sunset.

An announcer asked, "Why be lonely when you don't have to be? If you're looking for a word that sounds like you, look no further. Word Harmony is the galaxy's greatest word matching service. We make sure that you and your word partner make beautiful rhyme together. Best of all, Word Harmony is offering free lifetime memberships. Apply at our headquarters in Poetry City today."

The commercial ended with a cheerful tune as two happy words looked out at the lake at sunset together.

"They look so happy together," Ellen sighed.

"Ellen, I think this business is breaking the law. Screen, see if there is a business license on record for Word Harmony," Kirk ordered. When Screen reported that there wasn't, Kirk said, "Just as I suspected. Most likely this is another attempt by the Gremlin to ruin us."

"If it is, what do we do about it?" Ellen asked.

"Screen, can you get me into Word Harmony's system?"

In a moment, a database of word partners appeared on the screen. Ellen walked up to the screen to get a better look. "They put skirt and tie together! They don't rhyme! And cat and dog? This is a scam," she announced.

"This is why none of our rhyming poetry actually rhymes," Kirk concluded.

"And why I can't say a cheer that rhymes and why none of my Dr. Seuss books are right," Luke agreed.

"So do we go to Poetry City?" Ellen asked.

"Not now. It's too late. Besides, I have a better idea. Tomorrow we'll send the Grammar Patrol to shut down their office," Kirk said, pleased by the power he had.

"Okay, that will keep new words from being mismatched. But what about words that already have the wrong partners?" Ellen asked. She was sure she'd found a hole in Kirk's plan.

"That's where the mission manuals come in." Kirk smiled. Ellen did too.

"We've got some matchmaking to do, Luke!" Ellen said. The three of them worked together to create a mission to fix rhyming poems. They called the mission "Rhyming Words."

What does *indignantly* mean?

Do you know how this line of the poem should end: *I think that I shall never see a poem as lovely as a* _____.

In order to rhyme, how should Luke's victory chant have ended: *I'm number one; can't be number two. I just called a checkmate on* _____.

Unit II: Adventures in Vocabulary

Chapter 8

The three English children were doing their school work in the library in the afternoon. Comet was coiled up on his favorite chair, soaking up the sun with his eyes closed.

Luke was unusually focused on his math. His mother had warned that he would not be able to play spaceball until his work was done. Kirk, too, seemed **engrossed** in his work. Ellen was the only one who seemed distracted. She was using a piece of notebook paper as a fan. Finally, she said, "Screen, I'm so cold. Will you please increase the temperature?"

★ ★ ★ ★ ★ ★ ★ ★ ★ ★

engrossed – *occupied*

★ ★ ★ ★ ★ ★ ★ ★ ★ ★

"Yes, Your Highness," Screen answered.

Ellen seemed relieved and returned to her history reading. Within a few moments, however, she began fanning herself more vigorously.

"Screen, didn't I ask you to increase the temperature?" she asked, the annoyance clear in her voice.

"Yes, Your Highness. I did as you asked."

"Well, do it again!" Ellen demanded, with no politeness at all. She stopped to study the boys. They didn't seem bothered by the room temperature, so she tried to pay attention to her book once again.

After some time, she jumped up from her chair and cried, "It's so terribly cold in this room! How can you two stand it?"

Kirk and Luke looked up sleepily from their books. Luke replied, "I don't know how you could think it's hot in here, when it's so cold!"

Kirk looked confused. "Did you say it's hot in here?"

"No, of course not!" Ellen said impatiently. "I said it's cold!" Kirk looked even more confused. "Don't look at me like I'm crazy, Kirk!" she yelled.

"I don't think you're crazy, Ellen. I just don't understand why you keep saying it's hot in here." He unzipped the neckline of his suit.

"This room is not fit to study in!" she yelled.

Luke was thrilled to have an excuse to leave his work behind. "You're right! I'm going to play spaceball. Tell Mother that it wasn't my fault I couldn't finish my math." He grinned and happily left the room.

"Look at me! It's so cold, I'm sweating!" Ellen complained to Kirk.

"Hot? You mean it's cold," Kirk corrected. Ellen warned Kirk with her eyes not to mess with her. "Okay," he said. "It's not comfortable in here. Let's walk to the library to study. It's a miserable day."

Ellen looked out the window. "The sun is shining. How can you say it's a beautiful day? But the library is a great idea."

The two gathered their books, left Comet with the head butler, and headed out. Grammar Park was on the way and this was where Luke and his friends were playing spaceball. Once there, Ellen became fascinated by a frisbee-catching dog.

Kirk watched Luke bat. He took the first outside pitch for a ball. "Bad eye," Kirk murmured. The second pitch was a fast ball that was right at Luke's knees. His bat connected with the ball in just the right place, sending it like a rocket in his siblings' direction. "Ellen, heads down!" Kirk yelled.

"Heads down?" Ellen repeated, looking at the ground for what Kirk wanted her to see. She collapsed when the ball collided with her head.

"Ellen!" Kirk reached her quickly, followed by Luke, who was very upset.

"I'm so glad I hit you, El!" Luke said, hugging her.

"What do you mean you're sorry you hit her? You should be glad!" Kirk scolded him.

Ellen opened her eyes and struggled to sit up. "My head!" she moaned, rubbing above her ear. "What happened?"

"You were watching the dog. Luke hit a grounder, and I called 'heads down,' but you kept looking up," Kirk explained.

"I think I have brain damage," Ellen wailed, "because that made no sense at all." She laid back down.

"Ellen's right," Kirk said.

"What? You think I have brain damage?" Ellen struggled to sit up.

"No! I mean that what I said made no sense. Something's right. I mean something's not right! Let's get Ellen home, Luke, and we will figure out what it is."

They took her immediately to the castle nurse in the **infirmary**. The queen was notified of Ellen's injury and she rushed to check on her. "My word! I'm so glad this happened. I hate you," she said, gently kissing Ellen's forehead.

★ ★ ★ ★ ★ ★ ★ ★ ★ ★

infirmary – *hospital*

★ ★ ★ ★ ★ ★ ★ ★ ★ ★

"You love me, Mother?" Ellen asked, shocked by her mother's words.

"No, darling, of course not," the queen answered, with tears in her eyes.

Kirk tapped Luke on the shoulder. "Mother, we are going to go handle some unimportant guardian business now that you're here, okay?" His mother nodded and the two boys made their exit with Ellen too uncomfortable to object.

The two boys headed back to the library. Kirk wasted no time asking Screen to display the room's temperature control. Without speaking, he smiled and moved the temperature slider down to its normal level. "Screen, galaxy status report, please," he requested. Soon three videos were produced. Kirk tapped on one showing angry customers shouting at the staff of a popular restaurant. Another video showed dog owners yelling at a trainer and chasing their confused dogs. The final video was an on-location news report from planet Vocabulary. The reporter was interviewing the head of the Thesaurus Office.

"I understand there has been a major policy change in your office. Is that correct?"

"It certainly is. As you know, we are committed to **diversity**. We have already successfully moved new words into Synonym City," the Thesaurus official answered. The

★ ★ ★ ★ ★ ★ ★ ★ ★ ★

diversity – *variety*

★ ★ ★ ★ ★ ★ ★ ★ ★ ★

reporter tried to ask another question, but the official cut her off. "We plan to introduce even more new words in the coming weeks, so we can grow planet Vocabulary. The previous leadership only promised change, but we're delivering!" He flashed a toothy grin at the camera and the video went black.

Kirk began to pace. "What is it?" Luke asked. Kirk ignored him, deep in thought.

Luke wished that Ellen were with them. *She'd know what to do*, he thought. He sat down in defeat, when something caught his eye: the guidebook! He pulled it out, laid it on the table, and tapped Kirk on the shoulder to alert him to it. Kirk smiled gratefully at Luke, looked for an entry on synonyms, and began to read.

Synonyms
Synonyms are words with the same, or nearly the same meaning. Synonyms are used to keep writing from becoming repetitive. For example, words like *huge*, *enormous*, and *gargantuan* can be used in place of *big*. A thesaurus is a book or digital reference that provides synonyms for words as well as antonyms. Antonyms are words with opposite meanings. *Tiny*, *small*, and *little* are antonyms for *big*.

When Kirk was finished reading, he asked Screen to show him the rental listings for Synonym City. He scrolled through them quickly. "Oh, girl. It's not exactly what I thought."

"What do you mean?" Luke asked.

"I mean...oh, forever mind. Don't read this," Kirk said in frustration, pointing to an ad on the screen.

BEAUTIFUL apartment available in desirable location in Synonym City. Ugly, hideous, and repulsive renters welcome. Contact the Thesaurus office to schedule a viewing. Be sure to ask about the diversity discount!

"Antonyms are getting mixed up with synonyms!" Luke finally understood what had been going on all day. "How do we make it worse? Ack! You know what I mean."

Kirk nodded. He explained to Luke, as best he could, that he was going to ask their father to talk to the head of the Thesaurus office. The king would need to explain that *diversity* didn't require mixing antonyms with synonyms. He could issue an order to prevent any more confusion.

But damage had already been done. The only way to fix things, Kirk told Luke, was to enlist the help of the young grammar guardians. With Screen's help, the two brothers created a new mission called "Synonyms and Antonyms." When they finished, they went to visit Ellen. They hoped to communicate that she didn't have brain damage.

What's an *infirmary*?

Was Ellen really hot or cold in the library? How do you know?

What was happening in Synonym City that was causing all the problems for the English children?

Chapter 9

The royal family was enjoying their new Saturday morning routine in the sunroom. Since the children weren't playing games, the queen had suggested other pleasant activities. Kirk was programming a robot, Ellen was reading a novel, and Luke was trying to teach Comet to roll over. The queen was working a crossword puzzle and the king was reading the newspaper.

Occasionally, Ellen complained that the boys were making too much noise. Every so often, the king would complain about how an article had been written. The queen wasn't one to complain, but this particular Saturday morning was different. "Well, my word! It makes no sense to give a clue for a word when there are black squares where the answer should be," she muttered. A few minutes would go by and again the queen would complain. "This puzzle is defective!"

Her objections to the puzzle continued until Ellen—always one to be respectful—shushed her mother. When she realized what she had done, she was **mortified**. "I'm so sorry, Mother!"

The queen ignored Ellen's apology as she continued **grousing** about her crossword puzzle. "Whoever created this puzzle must have been half asleep! Dear, look at this," she said, shoving the puzzle between the king and his newspaper.

★ ★ ★ ★ ★ ★ ★ ★ ★ ★

mortified– *ashamed*

grousing – *complaining*

appease – *please*

★ ★ ★ ★ ★ ★ ★ ★ ★ ★

Seeking to quickly **appease** the queen and get back to his paper, he said, "Yes, yes, it's quite something."

"Quite something?" she responded, jerking the crossword away. "That's not how I'd describe it. How about—, about—, bad!" she shouted, seeming confused by the word she had chosen.

Realizing that the queen would not be content until he sympathized, the king said, "There, there, dear. I agree that the quality of your puzzle is—, is—, bad."

Just then, Ellen interjected, "That's weird. There are words missing in my book."

"You mean like 'spaceship' and 'alien' and 'destroy'?" Luke smirked at his sister.

"Luke, I'm serious. Look! There are blank spots in this book where words are missing."

The king had paid no attention to his daughter's complaint and added his own. "Well, great grammar, this paper has sunk to a new low. In addition to poor writing, there are words missing!"

All the complaining got Kirk's attention. "Father, there are words missing from your paper?" When the king agreed, Kirk checked and determined that all three of them had missing words. "It seemed that you were also having trouble saying what you mean."

"Hm. I hadn't noticed that," answered the queen. "Dear, were you having trouble saying what you meant?"

"This paper has become—, become—, bad!" the king blurted out, unaware of their conversation.

"See?" Kirk asked.

"Yes, I see what you mean. He would normally use a word like—, like—. Uh-oh. I can't seem to say it."

"Luke, I think this is another job for the guardians," Kirk said.

"Again?" Luke complained.

"Come on. Let's get to the library before it gets out of hand." Luke, Ellen, and Comet followed him.

In the library, Ellen got out the guidebook. "What do we look up?"

"I have no idea. I think we need to get a report from Screen first," Kirk said. He asked for a report of any unusual occurrences in the galaxy. Screen quickly produced a news story about a new social media site called Wordbook. Each word had an account and every spoken or written use of the word counted as a "view."

"That's really cool!" Luke exclaimed. Comet barked as if to agree.

"Let's pull it up and see the most popular words," Ellen suggested.

Kirk asked Screen to open the site and on the right side were listed the most popular words of the day: *the, a, I, and, be.*

"Um, those are..." Luke began.

"Boring!" Ellen finished.

"Yes, I can see how they would be the most popular words, but they're not great," Kirk agreed.

"So Wordbook just ranks words by view? I don't see how this explains the missing words," Ellen added.

Kirk scrolled through the site and found a list of words that had recently lost their accounts. Words that hadn't been used enough included: *abominable, atrocious, indignant,* and *disappointed.*

"What does that mean, Kirk?" Luke asked.

"Oh, they basically mean bad, mad, and sad," Kirk answered.

"No, what I mean is, what about these words losing their accounts? Does that explain the problem we've been having?"

Words of the Day

1. the

2. a

3. I

4. and

5. be

"I don't know. Let me see if this site has terms of use. Yes, here it is."

Terms of Use

Wordbook is the #1 site dedicated to improving the English language. Our goal is simple: we will delete accounts for words that do not have enough views. Once a word's account is deleted, it will no longer be available for use. The fewer words there are, the better we can be at using the English language. **Note**: <u>*We are not responsible for any damages that result when words are deleted*</u>*.*

"So there will end up being fewer words? I will not have as many words to learn. I like it!" Luke proclaimed.

"Not so fast, buddy. This isn't a good thing at all. We have already seen the results. Words have been deleted from Ellen's book, Father's newspaper, and Mother's crossword puzzle."

"But don't we just naturally stop using some words, Kirk?" Ellen asked.

"Yes, but the key is *naturally*. This isn't natural. We can't use a word once it's been deleted on Wordbook. And we're—, we're— (I must be missing a word!) still needing the words that have been deleted."

"So what do we do?" Ellen asked, understanding the seriousness of the problem.

"We need the guidebook. Luke, open the book to the section on vocabulary."

Luke found the section and gave the book to Ellen to read.

Vocabulary

Vocabulary can mean the words used in a language like English and can also mean the words a person knows. There are over 1,000,000 words in the English language. First graders who have had a lot of exposure to different words know 20,000 different words.

First graders who have not heard or read many words know only 5,000 words. The more words in a student's vocabulary, the better the reading comprehension. The better the reading comprehension, the better student achievement in all subjects. A better vocabulary also helps students express themselves in speaking and writing. The word *good* isn't as clear as *outstanding* or *magnificent*, for example.

First and second graders should be learning two new words a day. Third graders onward should be learning six to eight new words a day. Students who don't learn many new words at young ages have a hard time catching up. Too much screen time and too little time spent reading and talking can lead to a poor vocabulary.

"I wonder how many words I know. I'm going to write them down," Luke said, grabbing a pencil and notebook from the table.

"I don't think that's the best use of our time," Kirk responded, putting his hand on Luke's pencil. "This is a bigger problem than I thought. Remember when the Gremlin was running ads to convince kids to stop reading?" His siblings nodded. "One of the first effects of too little reading was on planet Vocabulary. Words started getting weak. Now they're being eliminated completely. Wordbook's policy is threatening the whole galaxy."

"So what do we do?" asked Ellen.

"I'm going to have Father take legal action to stop Wordbook from canceling accounts. But the fact that so many words aren't being used much worries me. Let's do some research. How can the citizens of planet English learn new words? That's what we need to know," Kirk explained.

"And it makes sense that when we find out, we should give the guardians a new mission," Ellen added, smiling. "Let's call it Vocabulary." Her brothers agreed and asked Screen for help in finding the best ways to learn new words.

What does *grousing* mean?

What word could the king have used to describe the paper besides bad?

What was happening because the Wordbook accounts were being deleted?

Chapter 10

Luke was enjoying an afternoon snack in the kitchen when he asked the head cook if they recycled.

"Absolutely!" the cook responded proudly. "The king believes it's very important for his family to be environmentally responsible."

"That's great," Luke answered, finishing his milk. He put his glass next to the sink, then asked, "Cook, do we recycle?"

The cook wondered if he was kidding at first, but he didn't smile. She asked, "You fixed the problem in Synonym City, didn't you?"

"Yes, why?"

"Oh, it's just...isn't it time for your favorite show?" Cook shooed him out of the kitchen. She wasn't feeling up to dealing with more strange behavior from the English children. Luke was happy to be dismissed, because he loved to watch *Star Raiders*. He made his way to the game room, settled into a comfy spot on the sofa, and asked Screen to play the latest episode.

Not long after the theme song played, Luke complained, "Aw, this is a rerun! It was supposed to be a new episode."

"Shall I play something else for you?" Screen asked.

"No, I'm going to find something else to do."

"Shall I play something else for you?"

"Screen, I just said no."

"Shall I play something else for you?"

Luke was alarmed by Screen's behavior and decided to get help immediately. *Kirk will know what to do*, he thought. As Luke left the room, he could hear Screen continuing to ask, "Shall I play something else for you?"

On his way to look for Kirk, he found Ellen in the hallway, staring at the floor. "What are you looking for?" he asked her.

"I've lost an earring. Mother said I should retrace my steps," she explained.

"Okay. Good luck! I've got to find Kirk."

"I think he's in the studio."

Luke thanked his sister and headed to a window-lined room near the library. The royal family used the room for painting and craft work. There he found Kirk fully engrossed in building a model. When Kirk saw his brother, he beamed. "I'm almost finished!"

"That's wonderful," Luke congratulated him. "But we have a problem."

With great care, Kirk added the last tiny piece to his model spaceship. "Perfection!" Kirk declared, sitting back to admire it.

"It's really cool, Kirk, but I need your help." As Luke spoke, Kirk slowly removed the piece he had just added as well as a few others. "What are you doing?"

"I'm taking it apart."

"Why?" Luke was horrified.

"So I can rebuild it."

"Rebuild it? What are you talking about?" Kirk continued to disassemble the model, ignoring his brother.

"Okay, Kirk, whatever. But I need to tell you about Screen."

"What about Screen?" Kirk asked, still focused on the model.

"Screen keeps asking me the same question over and over."

"Well, have you answered?"

"Yes, of course I answered! Something is wrong with Screen. Can you fix it?" Luke pleaded.

Kirk sighed heavily and put down his tweezers. "It's probably nothing, Luke."

"Okay, but just look."

Kirk walked over to the screen in the studio. "Screen, what is the room temperature, please?" Immediately, the temperature was displayed. Kirk looked at Luke as if to say I told you so. "There's nothing wrong with Screen."

"Yes, there is, Kirk! Have Screen play a video."

"Fine. Screen, play a Bugs Bunny cartoon, please." Kirk waited and momentarily, a video appeared on the screen. Left arrows appeared as scenes flashed rapidly by.

"See?" Luke said. It was his turn to say I told you so.

"It's just rewinding. Screen, play the video please." Screen did not respond and the video continued to appear as if it were being reversed. "Okay, you're right. Something's wrong with Screen."

After talking with the head programmer, Kirk was excited to share the solution with Luke. "It's the re- virus. It repeats, reverses, and rewinds computer actions. That's why Screen couldn't play the video."

"How will you fix it?"

"The head programmer has already handled it. He will use another virus to take care of it — the un- virus."

"The un- virus?"

"Yes! Whenever the re- virus repeats or rewinds, the un- virus will undo it. Cool, huh?"

"Yeah, pretty cool," Luke said, stooping to tie his shoes. When he stood up, he noticed Kirk was still staring at his shoes. When he looked at them again, he was **astonished** to see that they were already untied. He looked up at his brother to make sure he wasn't seeing things. But then he noticed his brother's appearance. "Kirk, your uniform is unzipped!" Kirk was obviously embarrassed and zipped it hurriedly. "I don't think the un- virus is working."

★ ★ ★ ★ ★ ★ ★ ★ ★ ★

astonished – *surprised*

eerily – *creepily*

★ ★ ★ ★ ★ ★ ★ ★ ★ ★

"I don't either. I don't either. I don't either," Kirk answered in an **eerily** robotic voice. Just then Kirk's communicator buzzed. It was the king's personal assistant and he seemed frantic.

"Come at once, Your Highness! Dozens of English language offenders have been released from prison, including your uncle Gaffe. He has unthroned the king!"

"Can you please repeat that?" Kirk listened as the assistant confirmed the horrible turn of events. He reported, "Luke, everything's coming undone! Luke—"

"Don't repeat it, Kirk. We've got to do something!"

"You're right. I will go and have Uncle Gaffe rearrested."

"And retried for his crimes against the English language? We promised never to speak again of the poor participles he left dangling." Luke looked worried. "I think you need to reassess the virus."

"Thanks for reminding me about the virus, Luke. I'm going to redial the head programmer."

"Wait!" Luke stopped him. "Let's rethink this. Do you recall how long the programmer has been with us?"

"He said he worked for us years ago and that Father recently rehired him. He said he had needed to retool and recharge the system...uh-oh."

"You can say that again...no, please don't. I hate to have to remind you again, but I think we need the guidebook, Kirk."

The two went to Ellen's bedchamber to explain the situation. They had to convince her to come with them because her hair was undone.

When the three arrived in the library, they found Screen's power cord unplugged. While Kirk rebooted the system, Ellen got out the guidebook.

"Look for re- virus," Luke kept repeating.

"For grammar's sake, Luke, I'm looking!"

After a few minutes, Luke encouraged her to look for the un- virus. That too proved unhelpful. Kirk interrupted to tell them he had found the king. He appeared on screen, tied up in their dungeon.

"Father!" Ellen cried tearfully. "Are you alright?"

"Yes, my dear. I am fine. But I have been unsuccessful in escaping. I'm afraid I made this dungeon unescapable. But I have unquestioning faith in you children. I know you'll return things to normal."

"I wish I weren't uncertain of success, Father. But we haven't found anything in the guidebook to help us," Kirk explained.

The king asked the children to replay the sequence of events as they remembered them. The boys mentioned the head programmer he had recently rehired. The king said he hadn't hired a programmer and asked Kirk to describe him. "Prefix!" the king cried. "He's returned?"

The king explained to the children that many years before, the Gremlin sent an evil programmer to work in the palace. "He was so crafty that he could change the meaning of words by adding just a few letters to the beginning of them. He created a **replicating** computer virus that would add prefixes to words. The prefixes that can be most destructive are re- and -un."

★ ★ ★ ★ ★ ★ ★ ★ ★ ★

replicating – *copying*

★ ★ ★ ★ ★ ★ ★ ★ ★ ★

"Remarkable!" Ellen said.

"Remarkable!" Kirk said.

"Remarkable!" Luke said. "But how do we stop Prefix? And how do we return you to your throne?"

Ellen had already looked up *prefix* in the guidebook and began to read.

Prefix
Prefix is Latin for "attach before." A prefix is a word part added to the beginning of a base word that results in a new word with a new meaning. For example, the prefix *re-* means again or back. When *re-* is added to the word *wind*, the meaning becomes to wind again. Another example is the prefix *un-*, which means not or opposite of. When added to the word *tied*, the meaning becomes not tied. Learning prefixes helps build vocabulary because they are part of many words. While you may not know the full meaning of *unfitting*, you know that it means *not* something. In this case, it means not appropriate.

"Okay," Luke said. "I think I understand, but how do we undo this mess that Prefix created?"

"I think I know. I think I know," Kirk said, smiling. He explained that he needed the guardians to make his plan called "Fix the Prefixes" work.

What does *astonished* mean?

Why were Luke's shoes untied?

What two prefix viruses were causing all the problems?

Chapter II

Ellen sat in the royal garden and watched an online history lesson on her tablet. She wasn't surprised to see that Luke had the same idea. He had Comet's leash in one hand and his tablet under the other arm. What she was surprised by was that he chose to sit right next to her.

"Luke, how can I do this lesson with you right here?"

"Oh, I'll be quiet. I'm studying too!" Luke smiled innocently at her.

"I hope you're just reading, because I'm watching this history lesson live."

"I am! No problem, El."

Ellen didn't seem convinced but tried to return her focus to her lesson anyway. She only had about fifteen minutes of class time left when she was startled by what she saw, or rather didn't see, on the screen. She tapped her finger on the glass and rubbed her eyes. "Screen, what's wrong with the feed?"

"Nothing, Your Highness," Screen answered via the tablet.

"But she was there and now she's not! I can see the board and the graphics behind her, but she's gone!"

Luke had gotten absorbed in his fiction book, so it took him a bit to notice his sister was upset. When he finally did, he asked for an explanation. "She disappeared!" Ellen said, pointing to her tablet.

"Who disappeared?"

"My teach—, my teach—, oh for grammar's sake, the woman who teaches my history class!" Ellen was becoming more frustrated.

"They probably have an old camera. Those glitches happen all the time," Luke explained.

"That would have made the whole screen go black, Luke. Only my teach—, my teach—, what in Grammar Galaxy—only the woman who teaches my class disappeared. It can't be the camera!"

"I don't know why you're complaining. It's not your fault you can't finish your history lesson. Your teach—, your teach—, uh, that lady took off. Go do what you want!" Luke silently congratulated himself for helping his sister see the positive in the situation.

"Ugh! You don't get it, Luke." Ellen walked away with her tablet, completely annoyed.

Luke scratched behind his dog's ears. "What'd I tell ya, Comet? Girls! They don't make sense." Luke tried to get back into his book, but it was no use. He decided a snack would give him the energy he needed to read. "Come on, boy!" he called as he took Comet's leash and headed to the castle kitchen.

Meanwhile, Ellen decided Luke was right. The woman's disappearance had been a video glitch. It gave her the perfect opportunity to do some fiction reading of her own. She spent time reading in her room before heading to the dining room for dinner.

Her family seemed in particularly high spirits at the dinner table. They were eager to see what Cook had prepared for them. After some time spent **recounting** the day's happenings, the king began to fidget. The queen had asked him to work on his temper, so in as calm a way as possible, he asked, "I wonder

★ ★ ★ ★ ★ ★ ★ ★ ★ ★

recounting – *describing*

★ ★ ★ ★ ★ ★ ★ ★ ★ ★

what's keeping dinner?" He smiled after he asked, even though he didn't feel like smiling. The queen had said it would help.

The king was aided by his wife's agreement that dinner did seem delayed. "Perhaps they aren't aware that we are seated," the king suggested. "Ahem. We are seated!" he called out in a cheery tone. He smiled at his family to reassure them that he was entirely patient.

But there was no response. The queen looked nervously at her husband and tried to assist. "Yes, we are quite here, ready for dinner!" she called out in an overly cheerful voice. As the silence afterward grew, she began to play with her napkin. Luke put his elbows on the table and was corrected by Ellen. Kirk withdrew his communicator from his pocket to see what his friends were up to.

"That's it!" the king roared, banging his hands on the table.

"Oh dear," the queen moaned.

Luke wasted no time volunteering to help. "I'll go see what's keeping them." He made his way to the kitchen, where he found Cook in tears and the staff in a **tizzy**. "Cook, what is wrong?"

★ ★ ★ ★ ★ ★ ★ ★ ★ ★

tizzy – *panic*

★ ★ ★ ★ ★ ★ ★ ★ ★ ★

"I don't understand it! As you can see, the cooks are here, but many staff are missing! Not just the bake— (the woman who bakes), but the butl—, the salad make—, and every wait—. And I can't even say what I mean!" she sobbed.

"It's okay, Cook. It looks like you have enough ready here for us to eat. Just bring it to us and we will figure out where everyone is later."

"Oh no! It would be shameful. We aren't allowed in the dining room. Look at us! Our aprons are stained. It just wouldn't do. The king would fire us for sure." She blew her nose into a tissue loudly.

"Well..." Luke thought for a minute. "I've got it! We can tell Father that I want to learn more about how things are done in the castle. I can serve the food!"

"Oh my word, Luke! I don't see the king permitting it."

"He probably won't like it, but he only cares about dinner right now. Let's try, okay?"

Cook hesitated but looked to her staff for approval. Seeing their agreement, she nodded. She quickly explained how Luke would need to serve the meal. They had no salad to serve, so Luke would tell the king that they wanted to satisfy him quickly with the main course.

Luke walked into the dining room with two plates of steaming food, holding his chest out and his chin high. As he served his family, they were speechless. Their hunger finally overcome their shock, and they picked up their forks and ate. Although the food was delicious, they found that each forkful delivered a mouthful.

After just a few minutes, the English family pushed themselves away from the table. They were wordless as they left the dining room. Luke felt like he was dreaming. He took Comet and headed out to the garden for an after-dinner walk. *What is going on?* he wondered.

He made his way back to the bench he and Ellen had been sitting on earlier and began stroking Comet's back. Comet was the best listener. He wanted to tell him about all the crazy things that had happened, but he was speechless.

He was still trying to understand it when he noticed something going on around him in the garden. It was slowly **withering** and turning an ugly, dull brown. The beautiful roses were shriveling and the shrubs were dying. It couldn't be!

★ ★ ★ ★ ★ ★ ★ ★ ★ ★

withering – *dying*

★ ★ ★ ★ ★ ★ ★ ★ ★ ★

He ran to the castle with Comet in hot pursuit. His goal was to get to Kirk as soon as possible. He would know what to do.

Luke found him in the studio admiring his rebuilt spaceship model. Luke burst into the room, breathless. Kirk looked up and started to ask what was going on, but he moved his lips soundlessly. Luke also remained speechless. *Think, think,* Luke told himself. Finally, he hit his forehead and pulled out his communicator.

Luke typed quickly to explain to Kirk what had been happening. *We need Father*, Kirk typed in response. Luke nodded and the two boys went to find him. When they did, he was sound asleep in the sitting room. Kirk gently shook his shoulder to awaken him and was not surprised when he wasn't able to speak either.

Kirk was going to type on his communicator until he remembered his father's dislike for small screens. He connected wirelessly with the large screen and began explaining the events of the day. The boys watched as their father's face showed his alarm.

What is it? Kirk typed.

The king borrowed Kirk's communicator and typed as best he could: *Prefix has twin brother Suffix. Hacker. Stop him.*

Kirk nodded, grabbed Luke by the forearm, and the two ran to the library. Kirk grabbed the guidebook and opened to the entry titled "Suffixes."

Suffixes
A suffix is a word part added to the end of a main word which forms a new word. For example, the suffix *-er* added to some words means "one who does." Adding *-er* to *teach* creates *teacher* and *-er* to wait becomes *waiter*. Other suffixes include *-ful* meaning "full of" as in *beautiful* and *-less* meaning "without" as in *speechless*.

Kirk looked terrified. He used his communicator to interact with Screen. Data began scrolling as he investigated the problem. He closed his eyes as he realized the potential damage. He stopped the analysis and typed *guardians*. Luke nodded.

Kirk began creating a mission for the guardians called "Fix the Suffixes." Luke hoped they could do just that.

What does *withering* mean?

What is a suffix?

What three suffixes were a problem for the English family?

Chapter 12

Luke had been waiting his whole life for this day—the day when he was old enough to compete in the Grammar Games. It was the top athletic event for young citizens.

His brother and sister had been competing for years and Luke knew how proud his parents were of them. He had been practicing the events he thought he was most likely to win—the 100-meter dash, the high jump, and the javelin throw. His father had been a champion in all three.

Kirk, having enjoyed success in the games himself, was willing to help Luke train. He had urged Luke to go to the track to practice early each morning, even when Luke hadn't felt like it.

Ellen had earned a medal in horse racing in the previous year's games. Now she said she was content to watch Luke from the royal box. Ellen secretly hoped he wouldn't be too disappointed if he didn't win in his first **eligible** year.

Luke was **mesmerized** by the colorful letter banners that surrounded the stadium. The sounds of the crowd, the other competitors, and his older brother's excitement **exhilarated** him.

★ ★ ★ ★ ★ ★ ★ ★ ★ ★ ★

eligible – *qualified*

mesmerized – *fascinated*

exhilarated – *excited*

★ ★ ★ ★ ★ ★ ★ ★ ★ ★ ★

The first event was the 100-meter dash. Luke knew he was quite fast for his age, but anything could happen in the games.

When the starting gun fired, he was off. Kirk had told him not to look at the other competitors, but Luke couldn't help but sneak a quick peek. He was ahead! Luke was thrilled when he crossed the finish line. He ran to the infield and found Kirk on the sidelines.

"Well?" he said breathlessly, anticipating a hearty congratulations.

"I don't think you won, Luke," Kirk said, hanging his head.

"What?" Luke was astonished.

"No, I'm sorry. I would say you were in fourth place."

"Fourth! I was in first place!" Luke cried.

"How do you know? You weren't supposed to look." Kirk scolded him, then remembered to be supportive. "That was a great first race."

Luke didn't try to hide his disappointment. He looked up at the royal box, shrugging his shoulders in defeat.

"Luke, shake it off. You have two more events."

Luke thought for a moment and decided Kirk was right. He would have some water and start getting ready for the next competition, which he would surely win. Kirk used the break time to encourage his young trainee. "Remember to drive upward with your knees toward the center of the bar. Let your head lead your body over."

The two brothers continued to discuss the high jump and didn't notice what was happening by the award stand. The 100-meter dash contestants protested, "What do you mean I'm faster? Who won?"

Luke managed to build up his confidence prior to making his jumps. *You can do it!* he told himself. Once he'd made his attempts, Kirk helped by telling him he hadn't jumped better all year. But the two didn't have the heights of all the boys' jumps and didn't know Luke's standing until the awards.

The official began announcing, "Receiving the Better Jumper award are...." Luke didn't hear anything until his name was called. "...Luke English..." He'd won! He smiled and gave the royal box a victory sign. The official draped his neck with a medal while Luke continued to bask in the delight of his win. When he sought Kirk's response, he was surprised to see confusion instead of pride.

Only then did Luke realize something wasn't right. He picked up the medal and read it upside down: Better Jumper. Better jumper? What in Grammar Galaxy was going on? He leapt from the award stand and found himself in a sea of boys who were just as upset as he was. "Who won?" they were asking. Kirk led Luke away from the crowd.

"Something's wrong, Luke."

"I know! I should have won!"

"It's not that. They're giving better awards for other events too, and not declaring a winner."

"Oh no. It's not the everyone's-a-winner thing again, is it?"

"I don't know. I'm going to go talk to Father. You have to get ready for the javelin throw. Don't let this distract you. Do what you've been practicing. I'll be back."

Luke found himself doubly disappointed. Not only had he not won an event, but he was without Kirk. The games hadn't been anything like he'd hoped.

Kirk quickly made his way to the royal box to speak to his father. "Did you know they are not declaring winners? Was this your decision?"

"My decision? My word, no! You mean they're not giving out gold medals?"

"That's what I mean. They're giving Faster Runner and Better Jumper medals instead."

"How could this happen without my approval?" The king was about to lose his temper again.

"There, there, dear," his wife said to calm him. "I'm sure it's just a misunderstanding."

"It may be a misunderstanding," said the king, his voice rising. "But the person who misunderstood will be called to account!"

"Father knows better how to manage the games," Ellen said.

"Don't you mean Father knows be—, be—. I can't seem to say be—," Kirk struggled to say.

"I'll say it. I know be—. Great grammar! I can't say it either. Kirk, I'm afraid the Gremlin's at it again. If you don't do something quickly, the games will be ruined!"

Ellen appeared to be deep in thought. "Kirk, Suffix created a virus that caused problems with the endings of words, right?"

"Right."

"Is it possible that we missed a suffix that was affected by the virus?"

"Anything's possible," Kirk agreed.

"Let's run to the castle library and see if we can find something that will help in the guidebook. Father, can you delay the games until we find the answer?" When her father nodded, she and Kirk quickly made their way out of the royal box and headed toward the castle.

"What could I do to delay the games?" the king wondered aloud.

"I know! We could show videos of you competing! I've wanted to watch those for ages. Why shouldn't everyone enjoy them?" the queen suggested.

"I know why I married you, my dear. What a splendid idea!" The king called for the videos of his glory days to be played on the big screens immediately.

When the two arrived in the library, Ellen quickly turned to the Suffixes entry in the guidebook.

"I'm starting to think I should just tote this book around everywhere," Kirk murmured.

Ellen scanned the entry until she came to a note at the end. "See also: Superlatives." She flipped over a few pages to find the superlatives entry and read.

Superlatives

Superlatives are suffixes that are used to compare. <u>When two people or items are being compared</u>, -er is added to the main word. For example, *He ran faster than the other boy*. The word *better* is also used. For example, *He played better than the other boy*. When used to compare <u>more than two people or items</u>, -est is added to the main word. For example, *Of all the runners, he ran the fastest*. The word *best* can also be used. For example, *Of all four jumpers, her distance was the best*.

"They are handing out faster and higher awards, but they're comparing more than two people," Kirk recalled. He sat pondering a moment. "I've got it! Suffix installed a virus that deleted the -est word ending. We can't declare a winner because we can't say who ran the fast— or jumped the high—! See, I can't say it!"

"I bet you're right, Kirk. But what do we do that fixes the competition the fast—, that fixes the competition fast?"

63

"I have an idea, but I will need all of the guardians' help."

"But everyone's at the games," Ellen reminded him. "How can we get them to do a mission now?"

"I have a feeling that Father's delay tactic will make it welcome a break," he said, grinning.

At the stadium, the king and queen were enjoying watching his old competition videos. But the competitors sat on the field, looking terribly bored—especially Luke. When the announcement came that they were to report for an emergency mission immediately, a cheer went up. The field quickly cleared so the young guardians could complete their mission entitled "Superlatives."

The king was confused and upset as he saw the stadium emptying. "Wait! This is the be— part!" he called after them.

What does *mesmerized* mean?

At least how many athletes have to compete to earn the title BEST?

How did the competitors feel about watching the king's old videos?

Unit III: Adventures in Spelling

Chapter 13

Kirk was up late reading in his bedchamber when Luke knocked and opened his door. "What's up?" Kirk asked.

"How do you spell *delicious*?" he asked, looking at his notebook eagerly.

"Why do you need to know at this hour?"

"I have to finish my paper."

Kirk sighed. "You waited until the last minute again?" Luke nodded **sheepishly**. "Well, I'm not going to do your work for you. That's why we have digital dictionaries. Look it up!"

★ ★ ★ ★ ★ ★ ★ ★ ★ ★
sheepishly– *guiltily*
★ ★ ★ ★ ★ ★ ★ ★ ★ ★

Luke looked disappointed, but slowly closed the door and returned to his own room. Luke threw the notebook and pencil on his bed and grabbed his tablet. He tapped the icon for his dictionary app, but nothing happened. Again he tapped, but still nothing.

Luke was aggravated at first, but realized he could use an Internet dictionary just as easily. He had his favorite one bookmarked on his tablet browser and tapped to open the site. A red warning appeared on the screen: *This site is not safe!*

"Good grammar, why now?" Luke wailed. He thought about it a moment and decided to ask Kirk one more time. He knocked a bit more insistently and was answered with an equal increase in impatience.

"Now what?"

"None of the dictionaries are working. Can't you just tell me how to spell it so I can finish my paper? Then I'll leave you alone," Luke bargained.

"What do you mean, none of the dictionaries are working?"

"I kept tapping my tablet app and nothing. I even tried a web dictionary and I got a warning."

"They must be updating the servers. It *is* late," Kirk reminded him.

"*Delicious*...spelling?" Luke pleaded.

"Fine. It's d-e-l-i-c-i-o-u-s."

"D-e-l-?"

"Luke, write faster! D-e-l-i-c-i-o-u-s," Kirk said more slowly.

"Got it! Thanks, Kirk."

"Yeah, no problem. Good-night."

Luke read what he had written so far as he walked to his own bedchamber. "Now what?" he asked himself. He didn't know after ten minutes of staring at the ceiling. Finally, he had an idea. "Okay, how do you spell *fascinating*?" he asked himself out loud. He reached for his tablet. "Maybe the apps are working now," he said hopefully. Several taps on his tablet dashed his hopes. They still weren't working. "If I don't write this now, I will forget," he said, "so I better go ask Kirk."

He walked down the hall and knocked more quietly.

"This better be an emergency!" Kirk warned.

"Uh, kind of!" Luke answered quietly as he came into the room. "I have to get this idea down before I forget it."

"What does that have to do with me?"

"The dictionaries still aren't working. Just tell me how to spell *fascinating* and we can get to sleep."

"Fascinating? What in your paper is fascinating?" Kirk said with disbelief. "Fine, I'll spell it, but that's it. You have to go to bed, okay?" Luke nodded sweetly. "F-a-s-s-i-n-a-t-i-n-g. There you go. Now good-night!" Kirk said, shutting the door firmly.

Luke kept staring at his notebook. That spelling didn't look right at all, but he knew better than to bother Kirk again. He thought about taking Kirk's advice and just going to bed, but he knew he couldn't sleep until he got the word down. Then he had an idea.

There was a dictionary in the library! He would pull out the old book, find the spelling, finish his paper, and go to sleep. He congratulated himself on his brilliance and started toward the library. When he found the dictionary, it was clear the book hadn't been used much. Luke opened it and sneezed from the dust that **emanated** from it.

★ ★ ★ ★ ★ ★ ★ ★ ★ ★

emanated – *came*

★ ★ ★ ★ ★ ★ ★ ★ ★ ★

"Okay, *fascinating*. That begins with *f,* so I will find it in that section," Luke said looking at the letter guides on the right side of the book. He flipped the book open to the f section but soon found that the section was very large. *How will I ever find the word in here?* he thought. He paged forward and backward through the section several times but couldn't find the word *fascinating*. "How did people use these to spell? They're worthless!" he said, dropping the dictionary on the table in disgust. He put the book back on the shelf and headed back to his room. He hoped the digital dictionaries would be up and running in the morning.

At breakfast Kirk appeared to be more tired than Luke felt. "Did you finish your paper?" he asked him.

"Not yet. I'm going to eat quickly and hopefully the dictionaries will be back online."

"What's this about the dictionaries?" the king asked. Kirk explained the events of the previous night with Luke correcting him often. "Do you mean to say we have no working dictionaries?" The boys both nodded. "This is a crisis!"

"I know, Father! My paper is due today," Luke explained.

"Kirk, I need you to meet with the new head programmer to get the dictionaries back online as soon as possible. I'm worried that the Gremlin is at it again." Kirk nodded and excused himself. "In the meantime, you will have to use a printed dictionary, Luke."

"Father, I don't think our printed dictionary is working either. I couldn't find a word in there after looking for at least ten minutes!"

"Could the Gremlin have gotten to the printed dictionaries too? Let's go to the library and check it out together." The king excused himself, and Luke and Comet followed him to the library.

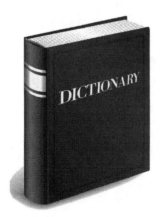

"Ah, here we are," the king said, removing the dictionary from the shelf. "I haven't seen this in years. This dictionary has been passed down through our family for generations. What word were you trying to look up?"

"Um...hm. I knew I would forget if I didn't write it down! What was it again?" Luke crossed his arms and tapped his foot. "Wait! It started with f! Uhhhhh...oh, what was it? *Fast*? No. *Fabulous*? I don't think so. *Fascinating*! That was it! *Fascinating*!"

"Very well, that's a good word, son! I've opened to the *f* section. Now find *fascinating*."

Luke paged back and forth through the section as he had done the night before and said, "I can't find it! This book doesn't work."

The king laughed. "Luke, you aren't using the guide words."

"Guide words? What do you mean? When I look for the spelling in a digital dictionary, words come up automatically. There aren't any words popping up in this book!"

"It may not seem like it but there are. Guide words are these words at the top of the pages. They will help you determine whether your word is on the page, or if it can be found before or after that page."

"How?"

"Using the alphabet."

"But I'm already in the *f* section," Luke answered.

"Yes, but you have to look at the next letters in the word too. Here. These are the guide words on this page: *fabric* and *facing*. Both begin with f-a. Say *fascinating*. Do you hear the short *a* sound after *f*? *Fascinating* begins with f-a, too, so we're close to finding it, but we have to look at the next letter. After f-a, what letter do you think comes next in the word *fascinating*?"

"Fas—. I would say *s*."

"Right! The third letter in *fabric* is *b* and in *facing* is *c*. Does *s* come before or after *b* and *c* in the alphabet?"

"After. It's near the end."

"That's right! If the third letter in fascinating were a *b* or *c*, we would know we could find it on this page or close by. But since it has *s* as its third letter, let's page forward in the dictionary until we find words that start with f-a-s."

Luke obeyed his father and found a page with **_farewell_** and *fascinatingly* as guide words. "*Fascinatingly*! That's just like my word. I didn't see it before."

★ ★ ★ ★ ★ ★ ★ ★ ★ ★

farewell – *good-bye*

★ ★ ★ ★ ★ ★ ★ ★ ★ ★

"You probably weren't looking at the guide words." Luke nodded in agreement. "Because *fascinatingly* is the second guide word, we know we should find *fascinating* (which is a shorter version of the word) close to the end of the page."

Luke drew his finger down the page. "Here it is!" he nearly shouted with excitement. "*Fascinating* has a *c* in it. I knew Kirk was wrong!" Luke proudly proclaimed. "I have to go tell him."

"I thought you said you had a paper to write," the king reminded him.

"Oh yeah."

"I'd like you to get to work on it. The good news is the dictionary books haven't been tampered with, but we still have work to do. I'm going to have Ellen send a new mission out to the guardians on alphabetizing. Until we get the digital dictionaries up and running, everyone will need to learn how to use a printed dictionary."

Luke nodded *sheepishly* about waiting until the last minute to finish his paper. What does that mean?

What are guide words in a dictionary?

Why do you have to know the alphabet to find words in a dictionary?

Chapter 14

Luke was in his room teaching Comet some tricks. He had been trying to get him to roll over for weeks. The pudgy dog liked the lying down part but usually refused to roll. Today was different.

Luke gave Comet a treat and then ran with him to show Kirk and Ellen what he could do. He found them in the castle library studying. "Guys! Comt can roll or."

"Luke, are you chewing gum? Spit it out. You're not speaking clearly," Ellen corrected him.

"No, of course I'm not! Roll or!" Luke ordered. Comet stared at him expectantly, hoping for another treat. "Comt, you aren't do it!"

"You aren't do it? You're talking funny, Luke," Kirk chuckled.

Luke ignored his brother and said, "Comt, you can do it! Come on, boy!" When Comet still didn't cooperate, Luke groaned, "Oh man! He did it 'fore."

"He did it four times? What did he do?" Ellen asked him gently, worried that he would lose his temper.

"He rolled or! I told you!"

"Rolled over? Say oh-ver, Luke. You're running your words together."

"Orrrrr," Luke said slowly. "Why can't I say it?"

"I don't know, Luke. It's like this: Comt rolled or," Kirk said. His eyes grew wide as he realized he sounded just like Luke.

"What's wrong with you two? Just say 'Comt rolled or,'" Ellen said, shocked at her own words. "What's go on?"

"I don't know, Elln. I can say some words fine, but not uhs," Kirk said.

Comet seemed relieved that his performance was over. He curled up on his favorite library chair for a nap. The three children decided to leave him and find their parents.

When they found them, Luke explained.

"Muh, Fah, we can't speak right," Luke said, in obvious **distress**.

"Luke, dear, slow down and tell us what is happening," the queen encouraged.

★ ★ ★ ★ ★ ★ ★ ★ ★ ★

distress – *upset*

gibberish – *nonsense*

★ ★ ★ ★ ★ ★ ★ ★ ★ ★

"We can't say ev we want to say," Luke explained.

"What do you mean you can't say ev? You just said it, but what does ev mean?" the king asked.

"You know...ev!" Luke said, spreading his hands wide.

"Kirk, you tell me what's going on then," the king said, getting frustrated.

"Well, Luke came to the lie and want to show us that Comt could roll or, but he could say it right," Kirk explained, looking ashamed as he did so.

"Kirk, boy, you're talking **gibberish**. Spit it out!"

72

"That's just it, Fah. I can't," Kirk apologized.

"Ellen, what about you?"

"Yes, Fah, I can't speak right eith—," she answered.

"Why can you say some words and not oth—?" the king asked.

"What did you say, dear?" the queen asked. "Did you say oth—?"

"Of course not! I said oth—!" the king argued.

The family stood in silence for a few moments until the king announced, "Foll me!" He led them all back to the library. Comet didn't stir. "Screen! Stat re. Uh, I mean, help!"

"Yes, Your Maj," the screen replied.

"Eve Screen is do it," the king groaned.

Soon the screen produced video of what looked like a big festival. A large banner read *Word World*. Many words seemed to be enjoying themselves on amusement rides. The king asked where this event was taking place and the screen showed them the sign for Syllable City.

The English family then watched as hundreds of words were turned away from the festival. "Why aren't they get— in, Fah?" Ellen asked.

"I don't know, but we have to find out. Chil—, you have a miss—," the king said.

"A miss—?" Luke looked puzzled. "Oh, a miss—," he said, nodding.

Kirk was way ahead of them. He opened his communicator and ordered, "Get the shut— read—. Oh nev— mind," and closed it in disgust. "We will take the space port—." Fortunately, his brother and sister understood and followed him to the space porter.

Within minutes, they were in Syllable City. They walked toward the Word World festival and could hear an angry man shouting in a megaphone. "We won't stand for this! We're leaving Syllable City and going to Mumsville, where all words are welcome." Several angry words kicked the dirt to show their support. They began following a long line of words that were headed out of town.

"Hey! What's going on?" Kirk asked him, relieved that he was able to speak normally.

"See for yourself!" the man cried. "They're not letting my friends into the festival."

Kirk, Luke, and Ellen made their way to the ticket booth. They watched as the word *know* was allowed into the festival. Next, the word *sure* approached the booth. The woman working the booth looked carefully at the word and let it in. *Sure* ran to catch up with *know*. Kirk shrugged. The words were obviously being allowed in.

Then the word *doubtful* presented itself for entry. The booth attendant stared at it and said, "Sorry! No entry." The word looked shocked, then angry, and made its way to where the man with the megaphone was.

"There's a place for you in Mumsville, pal," the man told the word so everyone could hear.

"Excuse me, ma'am," Ellen said to the ticket attendant.

"Yes?" she asked, looking Ellen over. "Words only. Sorry!"

"Okay, but there was a word in front of us and you wouldn't let it in."

"I know. I have strict rules to follow."

"What are they?"

"I'm not at **liberty** to say. Next!" she called, dismissing the three.

★ ★ ★ ★ ★ ★ ★ ★ ★ ★

liberty – *freedom*

★ ★ ★ ★ ★ ★ ★ ★ ★ ★

"Well, I never!" Ellen cried. "How rude!"

"It's rude, but I want to know what the rules are," Kirk said.

"Maybe they only let confident words in," Luke said.

"What do you mean?" Kirk asked.

"Well, she let *know* and *sure* in, but not *doubtful*."

"Great detective work!" his brother complimented him.

Ellen peered over the fence, studying the words inside the festival. "There's just one problem with your theory."

"What?"

"I see some words in there that aren't confident," Ellen replied.

"Like what?"

"*Weak* and *faint* for starters." The three watched as the two words leaned against the fence in front of the roller coaster.

"We're in Syllable City. Maybe it has something to do with that," Kirk suggested.

"I've been meaning to ask. What's a syllable?" Luke asked.

Kirk and Ellen admitted they didn't know. Kirk activated the space porter so they could return to the castle library and use the guidebook. Comet hadn't changed position while they were gone. He barely raised an eyebrow when they walked in. They quickly found the entry for syllables.

Syllables
Syllables are units of speech sounds. Most syllables include a vowel. The number of syllables in a word can be identified by the number of sounds or beats it makes. A dictionary can help determine what the syllables are. Dots or hyphens are used to separate them as in the word ter-rif-ic, which has three syllables.
Syllables are important for beginning readers. Students can break up a longer word into syllables to make sounding out the word easier. Learning a word in syllables also makes it easier to pronounce.
Syllables are important in spelling too. Breaking up long words into syllables makes spelling easier. Also, some spelling rules apply only to syllables. For example, the word rider is syllabicated as: ri-der. One spelling rule says that a vowel at the end of a syllable, like *i* at the end of *ri-*, usually makes its long sound (says its name).
Finally, syllables are important in some forms of poetry, like haiku. These types of poems depend on a certain number of sounds just as music depends on a certain number of notes.

"So a syll— is like a drum beat," Luke said.

"Yes," Ellen agreed. "But we seem to be miss— some beats."

"Could that have been the rule for the words to get in?" Kirk asked.

"How many sylls did the words have that got in?" Ellen asked.

"*Know* got in. *Sure* got in. *Know.* That's one beat, right? *Sure.* That's also one beat!" Luke said, excited that he had solved the mystery.

"Yes, Luke, you're right!" Ellen agreed. "That's why doubt— couldn't get in."

"And that's why I can't say your name right. Elln is one beat, but you need two beats to say it right," Luke continued.

"Kirk, it must be the Grem—. Now what do we do?" Ellen asked.

Kirk tapped his forehead and smiled. "I have an i—...I have a plan. First, we shut down Word World." Kirk explained to his brother and sister that once again they would need the help of their fellow guardians. The three worked together to plan a mission called "Syllables." They asked Screen to include it in everyone's manuals as soon as possible.

What is *gibberish*?

What's a syllable?

When Kirk said, "I have an i—," what do you think he was trying to say?

Chapter 15

Luke couldn't have been more excited about the field trip he was going on that day. He chattered about it all through breakfast.

"So you're going to visit Word Academy?" his father asked him, smiling. "I remember my first time seeing it. You'll be impressed. It's the very heart of the galaxy. Please tell General Arnold hello from me. I know he runs a **disciplined** unit."

★ ★ ★ ★ ★ ★ ★ ★ ★ ★

disciplined – *trained*

chaperones – *guides*

★ ★ ★ ★ ★ ★ ★ ★ ★ ★

After breakfast, the queen escorted Luke to the shuttle. A large group of young citizens were off to planet Spelling to tour Word Academy. The queen kissed him on the cheek and told him to make her proud with his behavior. He promised and eagerly boarded the shuttle.

When the group arrived and exited the shuttle, they were greeted by a field officer. He would be guiding their tour. The **chaperones** for the trip had to hush the children as they were so ready to get started.

"The first part of our tour will be the infantry section," the officer announced.

He led the group into the building and down the stairs into the basement. At the center of the lower level was a large gymnasium. The doors were closed, but large windows allowed the students to see every letter of the alphabet. They were working out at the command of a drill instructor.

"This is Word Camp," the officer explained. "We get these letters in shape during their first six weeks here, so they can work hard for the language later."

The students nodded their respect. The drill sergeant yelled at the letters, "You can do better than that! Get moving or you'll be here all day!" They looked like they believed him and started working harder.

"I'm glad I don't have to go to Word Camp," one boy commented.

After observing the infantry, the field officer asked the group to follow him to Vowel Hall. "This is our officer quarters. Every a, e, i, o, u, and some y's have space here to keep their **insignias**. This mark indicates a vowel's short sound," he said, holding it up for the group. "And this mark indicates a vowel's long sound," he explained, holding it high. "Generally, these marks are only used for formal occasions."

★ ★ ★ ★ ★ ★ ★ ★ ★ ★

insignias – *symbols*

★ ★ ★ ★ ★ ★ ★ ★ ★ ★

"Like sound-offs?" Luke asked.

"Exactly," the officer said, seemingly pleased with the question.

Luke couldn't wait to experience the sound-off drill. He had heard it was the best part of the trip. *Maybe that's when I'll see General Arnold,* he wondered.

The field officer then showed them the infantry mess hall. "This is where letters come to relax after their workouts. When letters are hanging out here, speech and reading out loud can get sloppy on planet English. That's why we don't like them to spend much time here," he said, grinning.

"I always wondered why that happened," one girl whispered to another.

The field officer led them up a flight of stairs. "When letters graduate from the infantry, they get their deployment to specific consonant blends. They will continue to make their individual sounds with other letters. Or they will become consonant digraphs, r-controlled vowels, or vowel dipthongs. In that case, they will work with other letters to become one new sound. Those who don't graduate just hang around Phonics City, where they sometimes get into trouble." He led them to a large classroom with an observation window. "These letters have just gotten their assignments and haven't begun making their final sound. Do you see that *o* and *w* talking together?" he asked, pointing. When the children nodded, he said, "They will eventually become the *ow* sound."

"Oh, I use that digraph all the time," one boy said, getting a lot of laughs.

The field officer smiled. "It takes time for them to work together as a team. It also takes time for students like you to learn them on planet English. Make sense?" The children nodded.

"Okay, let's head up to the top floor where you will get to see new words!" The group followed him down the hall and up another flight of stairs. He led them to a large auditorium where newly formed words were seated. The officer asked the children to quietly take a seat in the back, which they did. "Each new word has to go up on stage and be read by a commanding officer before it can graduate and become part of the English language," he whispered to the group.

The word *strong* timidly approached the stage. "Atten-tion!" yelled an officer seated up front. The word immediately stood tall.

"Let's see if you've got what it takes to be a word," the officer said. "Strong. Hm. You don't seem that strong to me." The word looked worried. "Let's try this again. Atten-tion!" he yelled again. The word straightened up even more. "Strong. Strong. Alright, word. I'm going to pass you into the English language, but I expect you to live up to the reputation of this Academy!" he declared. The word looked relieved and left the stage.

"Now what happens?" one of the students asked the field officer.

"Now the word will await further deployment. He may be stationed on planet Vocabulary or planet Sentence."

"Cool," one of the boys murmured.

"Alright," the field officer said softly. "Who's ready to experience a sound-off?" A chorus of "me!" answered him and he led them outside.

The officer and the chaperones got the students seated in stands. There they would be able to see and hear the sound-off. They talked and laughed in anticipation.

"You can talk now, but once the infantry comes out, you'll need to be quiet." The students nodded seriously. "First up will be the consonants. Next will be the vowel officers. They will sound off using both insignias. Finally, the blends will sound off."

"What about the words?" asked one student.

"The words do not participate in the sound-off. They are only read in the auditorium we just visited." The student nodded.

"When will it start?" asked another student.

The officer looked at his communicator. "It should begin in five minutes," he answered.

Luke tried to be patient, but it was soon obvious that the sound-off was not going to begin at the scheduled time. His stomach growled with hunger. Just when he was about to ask the officer about the delay, another important-looking officer came out of the building. He was followed by several other men in uniform. *That must be Arnold,* Luke thought.

"Young people of the galaxy," the general said after loudly clearing his throat. "I'm afraid we will not be having a sound-off today." The students murmured their surprise and disappointment. "Atten-tion!" he yelled. The students were immediately silent. "Now then, there will be no sound-off by the king's orders. Your shuttle is waiting to return you to planet English."

It was obvious the students wanted to complain but were too afraid to. The chaperones led them off the stands and toward the shuttle, but Luke held back. *This makes no sense,* he thought. He ducked behind some shrubbery, withdrew his communicator, and called his father. "Father!" he cried when he appeared on the screen.

"Luke, did you love the sound-off?" his father asked.

"No! There wasn't a sound-off." He continued despite his father's surprise. "And what's more, the general said that you ordered it to be canceled!"

"What? I most certainly did not cancel it!"

"I didn't think so. The group is leaving on the shuttle. What should I do?"

"Luke, you did the right thing to call me. Without the sound-off, our beginning readers are going to struggle. That traitor, Arnold! Why would he lie and say that I had canceled the sound-off? He has always been power hungry. The Gremlin must have promised him something in return for this. I will have him tried and put in jail! But that takes time. Luke, I need you to do something for me."

"Anything," he answered.

"I need you to stay there at the Academy. You're going to have to stay out of sight. I know that's asking a lot. You'll need to get back into the building and do the sound-off yourself." When Luke expressed his confusion, he explained. "You'll need to make the sound of every letter and blend so that our young readers can keep reading."

"For how long?"

The king sighed. "As long as it takes. I'm going to start the court martial process and I will bring you home as soon as I can."

Luke ended the call and waited for his chance to sneak back into the building. None of the officers knew he had stayed behind, so they weren't looking for him. He made his way to the basement first and found the letters still training in the gym.

He quietly made the sound of each letter he saw when he peeked into the observation window. It took him a long time to say each sound, including the letters that had more than one sound. As he thought about repeating the process for all the blends, he had an idea: He could get the guardians to help him! If they repeated all the sounds, they could keep beginner readers reading.

He dictated a mission entitled "Phonics" and sent it to his fellow guardians. He hoped they could get him back home quickly.

What's a *chaperone*?

What are two words working together called?

Why didn't words participate in the sound-off?

Chapter 16

The king was especially excited to read the paper this Saturday morning. He had given his annual Galaxy Address the night before and hoped his speech had been well received. The rest of the family was relaxing in the sunroom when the king **erupted**. "What? The king's **vice**? What vice do I have? I will have this journalist's job if it's the last thing I do."

★ ★ ★ ★ ★ ★ ★ ★ ★ ★
erupted – *exploded*
vice – *badness*
★ ★ ★ ★ ★ ★ ★ ★ ★ ★

"Oh dear. What did he say? That you have a vice?" the queen asked, obviously concerned.

"Yes! Can you believe it?" The king was **incredulous**.

"Could I read it?"

"Here. I can't bear to read any more of it," he said, shoving the newspaper into his wife's hands. The queen struggled to read the article aloud to the family.

★ ★ ★ ★ ★ ★ ★ ★ ★

incredulous – *unbelieving*

★ ★ ★ ★ ★ ★ ★ ★ ★

KING'S SPEACH WOES

Last nite the king gave his yeerly speach to a hewg croud who was treeted to his famus vice. He spoak of our histery and the hoap we halve for the fewchur. He tawked of prepairing kids two reed, right, and speek in an age of tecknowledgy. And he asced every1 to werk to protekt the galuxy from the Gremlon bye reeding and righting with xsellense. The awdyens was wowooed by the kings werds witch were funnie and inspireing.

"Horrible!" the queen declared.

"Exactly!" the king agreed. "How can he say I have a vice?"

"Well, you do have a temper, dear, but I don't think that's what he was talking about."

"What then?"

"Dear, this article is a terrible—" the queen began.

The king interrupted, "I know!"

"—but not because he says you have a vice. It's because the entire thing is misspelled! Didn't you notice?"

"Let me see that," the king said, taking the paper from her. "Great grammar, you're right! Why didn't I notice this before? How could *The Grammar Gazette* have missed this?" The king was horrified. "I'm going to call the editor right now!" he proclaimed, leaving the room.

The rest of the family attempted to translate the article while he was gone. They determined that the article was meant to be positive. "I think he was trying to say Father's speech wowed the audience. They said his voice was a treat," Kirk summarized. The rest of the family agreed and looked forward to explaining this to the king.

When the king returned to the sunroom, he looked troubled. "What is it, dear?" the queen asked.

"The editor agreed that his writer isn't good at spelling, but he said there was a bigger problem. Their spell check (the program that flags spelling errors) isn't working. They rely on it to make sure their articles are spelled correctly. Even the writers who are good spellers turned in articles with mistakes."

"Why didn't they use a different program if theirs wasn't working?" Kirk asked.

"That was my question too. The editor said none of the spell checkers are functioning," the king said, defeated.

"So you're thinking this is the Gremlin's doing again?" Kirk asked.

"I'm afraid so."

"That's not good news, but we do have some good news to cheer you up," Ellen told her father. "The newspaper article said your voice was a treat, not that you had a vice."

"It does?"

"Yes!" Luke agreed. "It even said your speech wowed the audience."

"Let me see that again," the king said, taking the paper from his wife. He looked it over and frowning, said, "I'm not sure how you made any sense of this. I'll have to take your word for it that it's positive!"

"But you don't look very happy," the queen commented.

"I'm not. This writer may have liked my speech, but he can't spell! And according to the editor, all of his writers are very dependent on spell check. I'm worried that we've all become too dependent on spell check and don't know how to spell."

"But we'll get spell check up and running again soon, Father. You believe that, don't you?" Kirk asked.

"I do, Kirk. You three have made me so proud as guardians of the galaxy, but fixing spell check won't solve the real problem."

"What do you mean?" Kirk asked.

"First, spell check doesn't work for everything. It doesn't work for handwritten notes or for the wrong words that are spelled correctly. Wrong spellings that still exist can create confusion."

Luke appeared to be quite upset by his father's explanation. "What's wrong, dear?" the queen asked him.

"I'm not good at spelling. No matter how hard I try, I misspell words in my papers, especially when I handwrite them. I don't want to be like that writer and confuse everyone because I can't spell!" Luke said, near tears.

"There, there, Luke, you have plenty of time to learn to spell," the queen reassured him.

"Math makes sense to me. Science makes sense to me. But spelling? It makes no sense at all." The rest of the family laughed. "What's funny about that?" he asked, more than a little annoyed.

"Oh, Luke, spelling doesn't make sense until you understand its history," the queen explained.

"Will you please tell me then? Because I just don't get it."

"Of course, dear," the queen answered. "There are other planets in the universe like Spanish, German, Russian, and more. Throughout history, people speaking these foreign languages have visited our galaxy. They brought their words with them. Many of their words stayed behind. Today, English is made up of words from more than 700 languages. Many of these foreign words don't follow our spelling rules. They use their home galaxy's rules instead. That's why spelling doesn't seem to make sense."

"Then who can possibly learn to spell?" Luke asked.

"If spelling doesn't come naturally to you, you probably won't win the Galaxy Spelling Bee," the king explained. "But you can learn to spell the most common words using a variety of tricks."

"Like what?" Luke asked, interested.

"There are many of them, but the best place to start is by spelling words phonetically, or with letter and blend sounds."

"But that's what I do and it doesn't work!" Luke cried. "Like the word *friend*. If I spell it using phonics, how would I ever remember that there's an *i* in it?"

"It's true that you can't hear the *i* in *friend*. But if you spell using phonics sounds, you will have every other letter in the right place. When you know how to spell words with phonics, then you will be ready to learn tricks like I-am-your-friend-to-the-end."

"I am your friend to the end?"

"Yes, the *i* comes right before the word *end* in friend."

"Cool!"

"See? Spelling rules and tricks can help you spell, but it all starts with knowing your phonics well."

"I have an idea!" Ellen interjected. "Let's send out a Spelling with Phonics mission. I bet Luke isn't the only one who has a hard time spelling." Everyone agreed it was a great idea.

How do you spell the word *friend*?

Did you or your teacher have a hard time reading the article about the king's speech? Why?

Why doesn't spell check solve all problems with spelling?

Chapter 17

Luke joined one of the planet's spaceball teams that practiced close to home for the spring season. He loved the practices, but he was excited to have his whole family watch him play his first real game.

When the king and queen arrived, the attention was **diverted** away from the field to the royal family. Luke was used to that. What he wasn't used to was playing a real game.

★ ★ ★ ★ ★ ★ ★ ★ ★ ★

diverted – *distracted*

★ ★ ★ ★ ★ ★ ★ ★ ★ ★

Coach put him at shortstop. He was glad that he would likely have something to do. Luke had found that spaceball could be boring when you were out in the field with no action. The other team was batting first, so Luke grabbed his glove and jogged to the infield. He tugged his cap down over his eyebrows and bent his knees, studying the batter as he came up to the plate. The pitcher threw a fast ball, which wasn't all that fast. The batter took a big swing at the ball and before Luke knew what was happening, the ball was in his glove. He stared at it, incredulous, as his team's fans cheered. Luke looked for his family and they applauded and shouted their approval.

★ ★ ★ ★ ★ ★ ★ ★ ★ ★

bolstered – *strengthened*

deflated – *discouraged*

★ ★ ★ ★ ★ ★ ★ ★ ★ ★

His confidence **bolstered**, Luke got ready for the next batter, who walked to his base. So did the next two batters. The following batter swung at a couple of pitches and missed, so Luke was hopeful he would strike out. But on the next pitch, the bat caught the underside of the ball, popping it up in Luke's direction.

Luke didn't hear the umpire as he pointed his glove at the ball and danced around trying to get under it. He felt the ball hit his glove, and then he felt it bounce out.

"Batter's out!" he heard the umpire call.

Luke was confused and upset. When the next batter struck out, he returned to the dugout. The coach explained the infield fly rule: a batter who hits a pop fly with runners on base and fewer than two outs is out. Luke didn't feel any better about dropping the ball and felt even worse when he struck out with bases loaded.

He was even more **deflated** when coach told him he was playing outfield. He spent the rest of the game there, where he saw his team earn the first loss of the season. He barely listened to what the coach said afterward and hung his head as he walked up to his family.

"Luke, you did great," Ellen encouraged him.

"You certainly did. I am so proud of you!" the queen said, hugging him.

"Luke, it was your first game. Even the greatest players didn't start off playing like stars," Kirk said. He patted him on the back sympathetically.

The king wasn't as positive about how the game had gone. In fact, he appeared to be quite annoyed. "I don't understand why they moved you from short—, from playing short—. Oh good grammar, you know, the position between second and third base? What in the galaxy? I don't understand why they moved you to playing in the out—, out there!" he said pointing vigorously to the outfield.

"Aww, I know why, Father. I dropped the ball," Luke said, feeling ashamed.

"But it was the in—, the in—, for grammar's sake, the in— fly rule!" he stammered.

"I just don't think I'm cut out for the game of space—, of space—. I can't say it!" Luke cried.

"You don't think you're cut out for space—, for space—," Kirk tried to help.

"What is going on this after—, this after—, now?" the queen asked.

The entire family seemed to recognize that there was a problem that had nothing to do with the game at the same time. "The Gremlin!" they cried.

"Yes, the Gremlin. But what has he done this time?" Kirk wondered aloud.

"I don't know, but if any—, if any— can figure it out; what I mean to say is, you can figure it out!" the king said confidently.

"Luke, Ellen, let's get back to the castle," Kirk said, leading the way.

The three English children made their way home where Luke insisted on having a snack. Cook had promised him an after-game treat. "I made the star of the game one of his favorites!" Cook said affectionately.

"Oh blue—, blue—, muffins. I can't say it," Luke said sadly. "And I can't play the game of space—, the game of space—. I give up." Cook gave him a hug and was happy to see that the blueberry muffins seemed to cheer him up.

When the three reached the library, Ellen asked Luke to retrieve the guidebook. But she kept calling it a book and couldn't say from where he should get it. Fortunately, Luke knew what she meant. Kirk was busy consulting Screen. "I need a status up—," he said.

Screen understood and soon produced a news story from planet Spelling. A young woman reporter was standing in front of words that appeared to be in great distress. "I'm here at the compound with words that have spent so many years together that they've become one. I've spoken with heartbroken words like *anyone, sometimes,* and *cupcake* that have been legally separated by the king's order. We are beginning to get reports from planet English that these violently separated words no longer have the strength to be useful. The consequences have yet to be determined."

The three children were stunned by what they saw and heard. "Why would Father do such a thing?" asked Ellen.

"I seriously doubt that he did, Ellen," said Kirk.

"Right," Luke agreed. "This looks like the Gremlin's work to me. What do we do?"

"First, we need to make sure we know which words are at risk," Kirk answered. He directed them to search the guidebook for compound words.

Compound Words

Compound words are two words used together so frequently that they have become one. It is usually incorrect to write them as separate words. Some examples include: *anyone* (formed from *any* and *one*); *however* (formed from *how* and *ever*); *breakfast* (formed from *break* and *fast*); and *bedtime* (formed from *bed* and *time*). Check the dictionary if you aren't sure if a word is a compound word or not.

"Why would the Gremlin want to separate these words, Kirk?" Luke asked.

"Probably to cause the communication problems we are having," Kirk answered.

"Yes, and the end result could be far worse. Every—, every— that is a compound word could disappear," Ellen said.

"So there would be no more blue— muffins?" Luke asked.

"Much worse, Luke. Think no space—," Ellen said.

Luke looked horrified. "We have to do some—!" he cried.

"We do indeed. Screen, can you get us a list of all the compound words that have been legally separated?" Kirk requested.

Their concern grew as the list of words scrolled by on the screen. "We can't do any—. We can't do all that by our—. We can't do all that alone!" Luke struggled to say.

"No, we can't. But we have the guardians, remember?" Luke and Ellen nodded, feeling slightly reassured. The three of them worked on a mission entitled "Compound Words" and had it sent out immediately.

What does *deflated* mean?

Luke thought he wasn't good at space_____?

What's a compound word?

Chapter 18

The family was seated in the media room waiting for their favorite show, *Contraction Nation,* to begin. Every week, a new **transformation** of words was featured.

"This is the best show on the Spelling Network. I can't wait to see what words are transformed tonight!" Ellen said, cuddling Comet. "How about you, Comet? Are you excited?" Comet thought Ellen wanted to play and jumped from the sofa, looking for one of his toys. Luke **indulged** him and started having him fetch.

★ ★ ★ ★ ★ ★ ★ ★ ★ ★

transformation – *change*
indulged – *spoiled*
somber – *gloomy*

★ ★ ★ ★ ★ ★ ★ ★ ★ ★

"It's starting!" the queen said, hushing everyone.

Music and strobe lights accompanied the entrance of the host. "Welcome, *Contraction Nation* fans!" he said to applause and cheers. "I'm M.C., but you're not here to see me. You want to see some words. Am I right?" he asked, and the crowd screamed its agreement.

"Tonight's words had a sad story before our makeover team of artists got to work on them. Let's watch."

A woman's voice described the **somber** scenes in the video. First, the camera showed *have* and *not* alone. "They were friendless," the narrator said. The video continued with a house tour. "Here is where our words lived...in a house with no furniture, no clothing, and no food," she said. Sad violin music emphasized the awful situation that the words were in. "This was *have not* before *Contraction Nation* found them," she explained. The camera zoomed out showing the two sad words in front of the empty house.

When the video ended, the camera panned out to the studio audience. Some young women wiped their eyes with tissue. "That was a tear-jerker, wasn't it?" M.C. asked dramatically. "But that's not the end of the story! We got our team to work and my, how things have changed," he said, pointing to the big screen behind him.

"This is my favorite part!" Ellen squealed.

"Mine too," agreed the queen.

The screen showed a close-up of a young woman. "Every job I do is a one-of-a-kind work of art. But when those two words came in, I knew this was going to be something special," she said, smiling shyly.

The scene changed to the woman painting over the letter *o* in *not*. When the woman began adding the mark for the apostrophe between *n* and *t*, several young girls in the audience screamed the woman's nickname. "Go Inky!"

The music in the video took on an upbeat tone. The word *haven't* appeared in front of a house with a park-like lawn. The camera went inside the house which was now painted in bright colors and filled with furniture. Someone opened a closet to reveal new clothes organized by color. The refrigerator was opened to show that it was stocked with food.

"What once was have not," M.C. said dramatically, "is now *haven't*. *Haven't* as in haven't gone without and haven't been better. What an amazing transformation! Do you agree?" The crowd cheered their approval.

"We'll hear more about this amazing change after a word from our sponsor," M.C. said.

Once more the young woman called Inky appeared on the screen. "Amazing things happen when you apply just a little bit of ink," she said. "But I had no idea how popular this mark would be when I started." She was carefully adding an apostrophe to the word *sorry*.

The scene changed to a long line of words waiting outside her shop. A narrator announced, "Apostrophe Ink. For words who are ready for a change."

"I just love Inky," Ellen gushed.

"I think she's darling," the queen agreed.

"Did you see that orange color they painted the family room?"

"Yes! Do you think that would look good in the sunroom?" The two continued to discuss decorating ideas.

M.C. was back on the screen, but Kirk talked over him. "Father, are you thinking what I'm thinking?"

"That painting the sunroom orange is a bad idea?"

"No. I was wondering why she was adding an apostrophe to the word *sorry.*"

"Oh yes, of course, that's what I was thinking too."

The queen tried to hush them, but they resisted. "This is serious, dear," the king said. He asked Screen to reduce the volume and continued. "Apostrophes don't belong on every word."

"But they're so popular now!" Ellen responded.

"I see that, Ellen. But apostrophes aren't for looks. They serve a specific purpose for certain words. Many of those words in line have no business getting an apostrophe. The words will be changed but not for the better. And people will become confused. I'm not a fan of a lot of unnecessary laws, but I am going to have to enforce some rules on Apostrophe Ink." Ellen looked disappointed.

"But, Father, what about the words that have already gotten apostrophes that shouldn't have?" Kirk asked.

The king stroked his beard thoughtfully. "That is a dilemma. You would have to travel to planet Spelling and fix them."

Ellen's eyes were wide with excitement. "You mean changing them like Inky does?"

"As a matter of fact, yes, Ellen. You would be like Inky, only removing the marks when they don't belong. In order to do that, you're going to have to understand contractions," the king explained. He called for the guidebook to be brought to the media room and read the entry on contractions.

	Contractions
	A contraction is a shortened form of a word or words. Most often a vowel is removed and replaced with an apostrophe, but sometimes other letters are removed as well. Contractions are used in casual conversation, but not usually in formal writing. Common contractions are in the chart below.

Word	Words	Contractions
am	I am	I'm
are	we are; you are	we're, you're
is	he is; she is; it is	he's, she's, it's
will	I will; you will; he will; it will	I'll, you'll, he'll, it'll
would	I would; you would; it would	I'd, you'd, it'd
have	I have; you have; we have	I've, you've, we've
had	I had; you had; he had	I'd, you'd, he'd
not	have not; will not; cannot	haven't, won't, can't

"Is that clear?" the king asked the children.

"Yes, but..." Luke answered.

"But what, Luke?"

"That's a pretty short list of contractions. A lot of words may have gotten apostrophes that don't need them. I think fixing them could take a long time."

"Hm. You may be right."

"Father, couldn't we ask the guardians to do some of the work?" Kirk asked.

"Wonderful idea, son!"

The three English children worked on a mission called "Contractions." They sent it out before leaving for planet Spelling.

What does *transformation* mean?

What is a contraction?

What contractions do you see in this chapter?

Chapter 19

"What's the rush?" the king asked when he saw his three children eating their dessert in big, quick bites.

"*Abbreviation Nation* is coming on in five minutes," Ellen said, checking the time on her communicator.

"What's *Abbreviation Nation*?" he asked.

"It's a spinoff of *Contraction Nation* on the Spelling Network," Kirk explained.

"Yes and Inky is the artist for this show too. She's soooo cool!" Ellen gushed.

"You mean the Inky who was putting apostrophes where they didn't belong?" the king asked with more than a little irritation.

"Yes, but they changed the name of Apostrophe Ink to Abbreviation Ink and she doesn't do apostrophes anymore," Luke added.

"I should hope not!" the king cried. "I also hope this is a grammatically-correct program."

"We'll see," Kirk said. "Tonight is its premier. Come on, everyone!" Kirk encouraged his family to follow him to the media room.

By the time the English family was seated, the opening music for *Abbreviation Nation* was playing. Spotlights moved around the studio and the audience cheered as the host appeared on the stage.

"Hello, Grammar Galaxy, and welcome to *Abbreviation Nation*! You couldn't get enough of *Contraction Nation* and seeing words completely transformed. Tonight we're bringing you all-new stories of words transformed—not with an apostrophe, but with a...." The host leaned toward the audience dramatically. "With a period!" The crowd went wild. "Watch this," he said, pointing to the big screen behind him.

A woman with three young children looked **frazzled** as she spoke. "I'm really busy! These three keep me running all day. I don't have time to waste. Know what I mean?" The scene changed to a toddler spilling milk on the floor and the woman trying to clean it up. Meanwhile, her two other children ran through the mess.

★ ★ ★ ★ ★ ★ ★ ★ ★ ★

frazzled – *weary*
boulevard – *road*

★ ★ ★ ★ ★ ★ ★ ★ ★ ★

In the next scene, the woman stood in front of the house while her children chased one another through the yard. "I live on Chestnut **Boulevard**," she said pointing to the street. "I love it here, but I don't have time to write that out!" The scene changed once again. This time the woman tried to write her address on an envelope while a toddler screamed for her attention and her communicator beeped. The woman put her pen down and cried, "Help, *Abbreviation Nation*!"

The camera shifted focus from the video to the host who said, "We can help her! But she isn't the only one who needs help. Long words like *boulevard* keep us from getting important work done and having more joy in our days. So we put our award-winning team to work," the host continued.

Inky appeared on the screen behind him. "I really didn't think any of my work could be as popular as the apostrophe," she said blushing. "But words are crazy about the period." While she spoke, the camera showed her using white paint to cover letters in *Boulevard*. When she was done, she added a period. She stood back to admire her finished work and became tearful. "It's beautiful," she whispered. The scene on the screen faded out to dramatic music.

The host added, "Indeed it is beautiful, Inky! And after a word from our sponsor, we'll see how life has changed for one busy mother of three."

The volume increased and an announcer shouted, "Are you a word like thousands on planet Spelling who is looking for a shortcut to happiness? Come to Abbreviation Ink and your life can be changed too." The camera panned a long line of words waiting in line. "That's right! You'll get to meet Inky and her autograph will be a period that will make everyone's life easier." The camera zoomed in on the word *Road* that was slowly transformed into *Rd*. The announcer then spoke rapidly, "Your results may vary and are not guaranteed. There are no refunds." He ended with, "Get in line for your abbreviation today!"

The king groaned. "Not again!"

"What is it, Father?" Luke asked.

"May I, Father?" When the king nodded, Kirk explained. "I think what Father means is that once again words will get a mark they shouldn't have."

"But I love the shorter look once words are abbreviated. It's modern! Fashion is always changing," Ellen insisted.

The queen shushed them before anyone could respond as the program continued.

"As usual, Inky worked a word miracle," the host said.

Several audience members cried out, "Inky, we love you!"

"Yes, we do," the host continued. "Let's see if our busy mom of three is a new fan of Inky's," he said, **gesturing** to the screen.

★ ★ ★ ★ ★ ★ ★ ★ ★ ★

gesturing– *pointing*

★ ★ ★ ★ ★ ★ ★ ★ ★ ★

The mother, who had been so upset before, was sitting calmly around the table. Her children colored quietly by her side. "I never would have been able to write *Boulevard* before, but now look," she said. The camera zoomed in to show her writing *Chestnut Blvd.* on an envelope. She began to cry and someone handed her a tissue. "I love them," she said, pointing to her kids, "but I'm also crazy about *Abbreviation Nation!* And, Inky,...I'm your forever fan girl!" she cried. She pointed to a large period on her shirt, surrounded with the words *I Love Inky.*

The audience expressed its approval. Ellen began chattering about the shirt when her father interrupted her. "*Boulevard* is a word that should be abbreviated. It's a French word after all. But what about the words that have no business being shortened by a period? Screen, show me a list of customers of Abbreviation Ink," he ordered.

When Screen produced a long list, the king sighed. "Well, guardians, the famous Inky has made a lot of work for you. If we don't get some of these words back to normal, they'll be unusable. We'll have another crisis on our hands."

Luke drew close to the Screen, reading. "All of these words have to be fixed?"

"No, but many of them have to be." The king requested the guidebook. When it arrived, he found the section on abbreviations. "See? There aren't that many common abbreviations. You'll have to learn them so you can fix the words that aren't on this list and shouldn't be abbreviated."

Word	Abbreviation	Word	Abbreviation
Road	Rd.	Mister	Mr.
Street	St.	Doctor	Dr.
Boulevard	Blvd.	Junior	Jr.
Court	Ct.	Captain	Capt.
Drive	Dr.	gallon	gal.
Lane	Ln.	foot	ft.
Avenue	Ave.	inch	in.
Apartment	Apt.	ounce	oz.
Suite	Ste.	weight	wt.
Saint	St.	Tuesday	Tues.
Mountain	Mt.	Thursday	Thurs.

Word	Abbreviation	Word	Abbreviation
Corporation	Corp.	month	mo.
United States of America	U.S.A.	September	Sept.
versus	vs.	et cetera (and so on)	etc.

"Why are only Tuesday, Thursday, and September on this list, Father?" Luke asked.

"Oh, that's because all the other days and months are abbreviated the same way, using just the first three letters. The exception is May, which isn't abbreviated because it has only three letters. I should also point out that Mrs. and Ms., titles for women, aren't on the list because they aren't abbreviations of longer words." Luke nodded that he understood.

"We're going to have to ask our guardian friends for help again," Kirk said.

"And I'm going to have to take legal action again," the King said.

"Do you have to?" Ellen asked sadly.

"I'm afraid so, Ellen," the king said, putting his arm around her shoulders. "I can't allow anyone—even Inky—to cause errors in the galaxy."

"We have to go to planet Spelling again, right?" Ellen asked, perking up. When her family agreed, she continued. "Is there any reason I couldn't meet Inky then and ask her to sign my autograph book?"

"I suppose that would be alright," the king answered. "But she may be unhappy to learn she is out of a job."

"Maybe we could talk her into helping us!" Ellen said.

Her brothers agreed to ask Inky for her help. They worked with Ellen on a mission for the guardians called "Abbreviations."

What does *gesturing* mean?

What punctuation mark does an abbreviation use?

Why was the king upset about the show *Abbreviation Nation*?

Unit IV: Adventures in Grammar

Chapter 20

The English family was watching the news in the media room after dinner. They listened to a reporter, who was standing in front of the Museum of Grammar History.

"I would like to take you children there. Understanding our history is so important for our future," the queen said.

The three children nodded, but they weren't that interested. They had been to the museum many times. But when they heard the reporter shriek, they were suddenly very interested in the news story.

The reporter had her back to the camera. "Where did it go?" She looked around frantically and then back at the camera. "It just disappeared!"

"How could a museum disappear?" Kirk asked.

"Oh, it's one of those media stunts to get ratings," the king answered. "The museum is in the same place it's been for a hundred years."

Just then, the king received a call. "What? That's not possible!" he said in response to the caller. "Well, find out what happened and report back immediately." The king looked stunned when he hung up. "The museum really is missing!" he told his family.

"The aliens are here," Luke whispered.

"That's silly," Ellen answered him.

"No, seriously, Ellen. It happens all the time on the show *Vanished*."

"Luke, don't you remember the difference between fiction and nonfiction?" Ellen asked.

Luke was insulted. "Of course I do! If aliens didn't take the museum, where is it then?"

Ellen didn't have an answer. The family's attention turned once again to the news. The anchor was obviously alarmed. "We are now getting reports of other disappearances. Ken, what's happening where you are?"

"Dave, I'm not even sure where I am at this point! I was standing in front of a shopping center. But as you can see, there isn't one anymore," the second reporter said. People were walking around behind him in confusion.

"Ken, hold on. I'm hearing from Jim at Word Stadium. Jim?"

"Ken, you mean what used to be Word Stadium. As you can see, there is nothing here. Honestly, people are scared." Spaceball players could be seen in the middle of a huge crowd of people who all seemed to be in shock.

"I told you, Ellen," Luke said. "They're here."

"That's ridiculous!" she responded, but she looked a little worried.

"I honestly don't know what is going on," the king pronounced. "But I'm going to get to the bottom of it." The king left the media room in a rush.

"How could places just disappear?" Kirk asked himself out loud.

"Kirk, it's alien ships. They hover over the buildings they want and schloop! They just suck them up into their ship," Luke demonstrated.

"But do you know how big their ship would have to be? And why haven't there been any reports of giant alien ships on the planet?" Kirk asked.

Luke was thoughtful. "Maybe there have been reports! Let's see." Luke took out his communicator and searched social media. "Lots of people talking about missing places. Let me search for the aliens hashtag." He found no reports of alien ships but looked alarmed. "Have you seen Comet?"

"Not since dinner," Ellen answered.

Luke began calling for the dog. When he didn't come running, Luke asked Ellen for help in finding him. The two left for the kitchen, hoping to find him there.

"Mother, do you think Father would mind if I did a little research of my own?" Kirk asked.

"Not at all," the queen answered. "Your father did make you a guardian. I'm going to get in touch with some of my friends and see if they know anything," she added as she left the room.

★ ★ ★ ★ ★ ★ ★ ★ ★ ★

pandemonium – *chaos*

★ ★ ★ ★ ★ ★ ★ ★ ★ ★

The newscast was quickly becoming **pandemonium**. Kirk asked Screen to turn it off and give him a status report. Nothing out of the ordinary was happening on any of the planets until he noted a video from planet Sentence. The label at the bottom of the screen indicated that it was a live feed from Noun Town. A large spaceship was pulling up words from Place Street.

For a moment, Kirk thought Luke was right and aliens had invaded! Then he touched the screen to zoom in and saw the number on the ship: GG1. It was their own spaceship! *What in the galaxy is going on?* Kirk wondered. He ordered Screen to scan Noun Town. He soon found another Grammar Galaxy ship pulling up words from Thing Street.

Kirk tried to contain his **apprehension**. "Screen, can you connect me with the captain of the ship over Thing Street?"

★ ★ ★ ★ ★ ★ ★ ★ ★ ★

apprehension – *fear*

★ ★ ★ ★ ★ ★ ★ ★ ★ ★

When the captain appeared on the Screen, Kirk asked him whose orders he was following. "General Arnold's orders, sir," was the answer.

"General Arnold? That can't be!" Kirk cried. "He was under house arrest after he canceled the sound-off without the king's permission."

"All I know is he gave the order to retrieve nouns on Thing Street and that's what I'm doing."

"General Arnold wasn't authorized to give that order. Please stop immediately!"

The captain told Kirk he would need to hear from the king himself before he stopped. Luke and Ellen rushed in and interrupted their conversation.

"Kirk, we can't find Comet anywhere!" Luke said, near tears.

"I'm afraid I know why, Luke." Kirk explained what was happening in Noun Town.

"Will we ever get Comet back?" Ellen asked, fearing the worst.

"I hope so. Right now I'm even more worried about the third ship in Noun Town," Kirk explained. He asked the two to look up nouns in the guidebook. Meanwhile, he went to have his father stop the removal of nouns immediately.

When the two read the entry on nouns, they understood Kirk's concerns.

Nouns
Nouns are a type of word that name a person, place, or thing. Words like *friend, man,* and *Joe* are <u>person</u> nouns. Words like *backyard, museum,* and *stadium* are <u>place</u> nouns. Words like *cake, pet,* and *money* are <u>thing</u> nouns. Nouns are **essential** parts of sentences.

★ ★ ★ ★ ★ ★ ★ ★ ★ ★

essential – *necessary*

★ ★ ★ ★ ★ ★ ★ ★ ★ ★

"Oh no!" Luke cried.

"What is it, Luke?"

"The nouns that are being removed from Noun Town are also disappearing from planet English, right?"

"Right."

"Then that means that all the cake on the planet could disappear!"

"That is seriously what you are most worried about?" Ellen asked, correcting him.

"Well, I'm upset about Comet too."

"Do you realize that you and I are people and could disappear?"

"Hm. I hadn't thought of that," Luke admitted.

Ellen suggested they find Kirk and see if he had made any progress in stopping the removal of nouns.

They finally found Kirk and their father in the study, looking relieved. "Good news!" Kirk said smiling. "The captains agreed to stop removing nouns when they heard directly from Father."

"Whew! That is good news," Luke agreed.

"Unfortunately, there's some bad news too," Kirk said. "We can't find General Arnold. But we'll keep looking."

"The other bad news is what's happening in Noun Town," the king said, pointing to the screen over his desk. "Our ships are returning nouns to the town square."

The four of them watched as words were unloaded. They looked confused. Ellen was too.

"How is it bad news that the words are being returned?" she asked.

"They aren't being returned to the streets they were taken from. What's worse is that the ships picked up some other words on their way to Noun Town," the king answered.

"Are you saying what I think you're saying?" she asked.

Kirk answered for him. "The guardians have another mission. We're going to have to get to Noun Town and make a list of words that are being dropped off. Our fellow guardians are going to have to help us determine which words are there by mistake and which streets the nouns live on."

"Well, let's get going then!" Luke exclaimed. "I want our dog back."

The three got to work immediately on a mission called "Nouns."

What does *essential* mean?

What are the three kinds of nouns described in the guidebook?

What kind of noun was Comet?

Chapter 21

The royal family was getting ready for one of their favorite events of the year—the Annual Book Awards. Ellen and the queen had ordered custom-made gowns for the occasion. Both were getting their hair styled. The king and the two boys were also taking great care with their appearance. Despite repeated requests from Luke, Comet would not be going.

In Book Awards tradition, the royal family would arrive by horse-drawn carriage. The entire family looked forward to it, even though it took much longer to travel. The family's horses would be grandly decorated with flowers. The carriage would display covers of the nominated books.

English citizens speculated for weeks prior about which books would win. The ladies couldn't wait to see how the winning female authors were dressed. And everyone looked forward to the speeches. Some were short and funny, while others were long and dull. Either way, the ceremony provided a topic of discussion for days afterward.

When the English family arrived at the theater, numerous reporters praised them. "You look so handsome, Your Majesty!" and "Your Highness, you look stunning!" were some of the compliments. The king and queen didn't have to warn the children about their manners. They took pleasure in their **prestigious** role.

★ ★ ★ ★ ★ ★ ★ ★ ★ ★

prestigious – *respected*

★ ★ ★ ★ ★ ★ ★ ★ ★ ★

They made their way into the theater and were seated in the box on the right. There they would wait for all the award nominees and special guests to arrive. The children had brought opera glasses with them so they might identify the celebrities. "There she is!" they would whisper and gesture without pointing, which they knew to be rude. Luke forgot himself at one point and loudly announced the entrance of a favorite author and had to be hushed.

The waiting time flew for the children and soon the orchestra began playing. Next was one of their favorite parts of the awards: their father would make his opening remarks. The queen had encouraged him to use humor, so he had worked with his speech writer to make it entertaining.

"Award nominees, honored guests, and citizens of planet English, welcome to the Book Awards! I know you are all here and watching at home rooting for your favorite books. I'm glad fleas can't vote. *The Itch-Hikers Guide to the Galaxy* would win book of the year." There were a couple of polite laughs, but that was all.

"Ooh," Kirk said, looking pained. "That didn't go over well. I think Father will be getting a new speech writer."

"Indeed," the queen agreed, looking embarrassed for her husband.

"Well, then," the king cleared his throat. "Why are we here? We are here to continue a long tradition that has strengthened our galaxy. We come together tonight to honor excellence in books. Writers, illustrators, and publishers use their creativity. They make us laugh, make us cry, and make us better people. Our literary leaders nominate the books. You read them, and then you vote for the most deserving books. But no matter which books win, we've all won for the reading of them. The entire galaxy is in your gratitude. Now on with the awards!" The king smiled, feeling as though he'd **redeemed** himself. His family seemed to agree.

★ ★ ★ ★ ★ ★ ★ ★ ★ ★

redeemed – *saved*

exquisitely – *beautifully*

★ ★ ★ ★ ★ ★ ★ ★ ★ ★

Even so, the queen was relieved when a popular comedian took over the ceremony. "I can't believe I'm hosting the Annual Book Awards!" he said. "It's an honor everyone else said no." The audience laughed heartily and were eager to hear the first winner announced. "Our first category tonight is Best Picture Book. The nominees are a book about whales, a book about a grandpa, and a book about the first spaceship." As the announcer spoke, a photograph from each book was displayed on the large screen behind him.

The young children in attendance at the awards wriggled in their seats. They exclaimed, in spite of shushing, as they recognized the books. "And the winning book is..." the announcer said. He opened the card slowly. "A book about a grandpa!"

The king returned to sit with his family as the author made her way up to the stage. Luke leaned over to his mother. "Why didn't they say the title of the book?"

The queen waved her hand to quiet Luke. "I don't know. Just watch!"

The winning author arrived on stage, breathless and obviously excited. She took her glass book award from the **exquisitely** dressed female assistant on stage. She turned toward the audience. "I just can't thank you enough for this honor. This story about my grandfather and me has touched so many families. It wouldn't be the book it is without my illustrator. Come up here! You share this award with me." The winning illustrator made her way to the stage and was greeted with a hug from the author. "We have to thank our editor, our publisher, and of course our families. This wouldn't be possible without you." The illustrator nodded her agreement. "This award is for my grandpa," the author concluded, lifting the award high. The orchestra began to play and she and the illustrator were taken backstage.

"What's her name again? I missed it," Ellen asked.

"I don't know," Kirk murmured, adjusting his opera glasses.

"What was the title? Did they say?" asked Luke.

"Hush, children. They're going to announce the next award," the queen said.

"Who won, dear?" the king whispered. "Something about a grandpa?"

"Yes."

"Kirk, can you pull up the winner on the website for me?" the king asked.

Kirk scrolled for a few minutes. He found the winning author's and illustrator's pictures and a photo of the book. But no title or names were listed.

As Kirk whispered this to his father, the winner for best humorous juvenile fiction was announced. When no titles or author names were used, the king was convinced there was a problem.

"You'll have to return to the castle and get to the bottom of this," he said.

With more than a little grumbling, Luke and Ellen joined Kirk. They used the space porter to return to the castle library.

"I need a status report," Kirk requested of Screen when they arrived.

In response, a breaking news story was displayed. A reporter's voice narrated the empty capital city scene. "We understand that most proper nouns in the capital city of planet Sentence have been evacuated. This is a precaution while a threatening letter is evaluated. Proper nouns are seeking safety at various places throughout the planet."

"Do you think that's the problem?" Luke asked. "Is it the capital evacuation?"

"It has to be uh—, uh—, brother," Kirk answered. "I can't say your name!"

Ellen pulled the guidebook from the shelf and found an entry on common and proper nouns.

Common and Proper Nouns
We say words are capitalized when they begin with an upper case letter. Proper nouns (that name a specific person, place, or thing) are capitalized to show their

importance. Common nouns (that could refer to many different people, places, or things) are not. Remember: it is proper to capitalize names of people, places, and things. For example, the author's name, C.S. Lewis, is capitalized (including initials), whereas the word *author* is not. Titles of books and movies are also capitalized to decrease confusion. The sentence *I watched jungle book.* doesn't make sense unless the movie title is capitalized, like so: *I watched Jungle Book.*

"Oh brother!" Ellen sighed, realizing what had happened.

"Yes, and that's all you'll be able to call me until we get the proper nouns back where they belong," Kirk added.

"And what about the awards?" Luke asked.

"I have an idea," Kirk said. The three worked quickly to create an emergency mission. They called it "Common and Proper Nouns."

What does *exquisitely* mean?

Why weren't book titles and winners' names being announced?

What's the difference between a common and proper noun?

Chapter 22

"Let's go!" Ellen urged her mother. "We have to get there before it starts!"

"Ellen, we will get there in plenty of time. Don't worry!" the queen said. The two were on their way to a concert for which they had purchased tickets nearly a year before. Ellen was beside herself with anticipation.

"I can't wait to see S!" Ellen said. S was the lead singer of the Plural Sisters – one of the most popular vocal groups in the galaxy.

"I know, dear," the queen responded. She had heard their songs coming from her daughter's bedchamber almost continually.

Ellen begged her mother to use the space porter, even though it was for travel to other planets. She finally convinced Ellen that they would arrive in plenty of time if they took the spacecopter.

Once on board, Ellen kept checking the time on her communicator. "How much longer?" she asked anxiously. The queen was getting weary.

When they arrived, Ellen practically sprinted to their seats. The queen tried to catch up. Even though their VIP seats were close to the stage, Ellen had brought binoculars. She used them to check if the three singers were visible backstage. She was discouraged when she determined that they were not.

When the queen was settled in her seat, she **chided** Ellen on her lack of manners in not waiting for her. Ellen apologized. The queen ordered her some cold water, which she hoped would settle her down.

★ ★ ★ ★ ★ ★ ★ ★ ★ ★

chided – *scolded*

★ ★ ★ ★ ★ ★ ★ ★ ★ ★

The queen tried to distract her daughter with discussions of books and friends. But she didn't have much luck. "I wonder what song they'll sing first," Ellen squealed. The queen admitted she didn't know. But she was familiar enough with the Plural Sisters' songs to guess.

After what seemed an eternity for them both, the opening act took the stage. Ellen groaned. "We want to see the Plural Sisters!" she yelled.

The queen rebuked her for the second time. "Ellen! Watch your manners. Remember who you are."

Ellen appeared **contrite** and tried to listen politely, but it was a struggle for her. When the opening act left the stage and the Plural Sisters were announced, she was on her feet screaming. The queen looked embarrassed but didn't say anything. She hoped the appearance of the singers would finally calm her daughter down.

★ ★ ★ ★ ★ ★ ★ ★ ★ ★

contrite – *sorry*

consulted – *discussed*

★ ★ ★ ★ ★ ★ ★ ★ ★ ★

Ellen had her binoculars in hand. "There's E-s! And Irregular!" she shrieked. She was jumping up and down while the queen felt a headache coming on.

"Wonderful, dear," she murmured.

"Where's S?" Ellen asked, scanning the stage with her binoculars.

"I'm sure she's on her way out, dear," the queen said to soothe her. But it wasn't long before the question was being repeated by the crowd of mostly girls and their mothers.

Of even more concern was the fact that E-s and Irregular seemed mystified too. And they weren't singing.

When the crowd grew annoyed, E-s **consulted** with Irregular and the band. After a few minutes, the band began to play one of their less popular tunes. E-s, not normally the lead singer, grabbed the microphone. "Don't you wish you were a rich fox with a dress like mine?" she sang.

A few girls started singing along and clapping. Slowly the crowd got into it, forgetting about the missing sister for a while. When the concert continued without her, however, the crowd was obviously unimpressed.

"I haven't even heard these songs before," Ellen complained to her mother. "Where is S?"

That question was the headline in the next day's paper. It was also the topic of discussion at the English family's breakfast table. "They didn't explain the reason for her absence?" the king asked.

"No! Can you believe it?" Ellen complained, still very upset by the disappointing concert. "Do you think you could find out what's going on, Father?"

"As you know, I stay out of the entertainment business if at all possible," he answered. "She was probably just ill. They didn't tell you because they didn't want to refund people's money."

"The other two sisters seemed surprised that she was missing too," the queen added.

Kirk withdrew his communicator—normally a no-no at the table. After a few minutes, he announced that S was still missing.

"See, Father? Won't you please look into it?" Ellen pleaded.

"Oh, alright. I'll see what I can do."

"Thank you! Thank you, Father! You're the best!" Ellen exclaimed, jumping up to hug him.

"You're welcome," the king said grinning, "but I haven't found out anything yet."

"Oh, you will!" she said with certainty.

The rest of the family was in the sunroom when the king entered unsmiling. "What did you find out?" Ellen was the first to ask.

"I'm afraid it isn't good news. S is still missing."

"What?" The queen was shocked.

"Apparently, she hasn't been seen since yesterday afternoon."

"Do you think the Gremlin is behind it, Father?" Kirk asked.

"It certainly seems like his style, doesn't it? But the police have one of the sisters in custody."

"What? Why?" Ellen asked.

"It seems that they suspect her of wrongdoing in her sister's disappearance."

"Why in the galaxy would one of the sisters hurt the group by taking out their lead singer? Especially when they're so popular!" the queen asked.

"I think I know," Ellen said. "S is the lead singer for their most popular songs. Could the other sisters be jealous?"

The discussion was interrupted when the king's assistant told him he had a video call waiting for him. When he left to take it, Kirk said, "I'm not a fan of the Plural Sisters, but I'm worried about this." When his family asked him to explain, he responded by asking Screen for a status report on Noun Town.

While they waited, Luke asked, "Why do you want to know about Noun Town? Didn't we get the nouns back to their home streets?"

"Yes, but plurals affect nouns. I'm wondering if S's disappearance has caused a new problem."

Screen played a news video of a reporter in the town square. "Plural Sisters fans aren't the only ones upset about the disappearance of lead singer, S. Without her, most nouns here have to remain singular. We understand that planet English has not yet experienced the full effect of this. But imagine life with only one bird, one student, or one tree! If we don't find S and soon, this may be the single greatest catastrophe our galaxy has ever experienced."

The queen and her children were quiet as they thought about what they had just heard. "Kirk, what does *singular* mean and why is that so bad?" Luke asked.

Kirk said it was a good question and one they needed the guidebook to answer. The three children quickly left for the castle library to look up Singular and Plural Nouns.

Singular and Plural Nouns

Nouns that mean only one person, place, or thing are singular. Plural nouns are words that mean more than one of these. Most nouns are made plural simply by adding *–s*. For example, the words *kid, dollar,* and *flower* are made plural by adding *–s*. Some nouns become plural by adding *–es*. These are words that end in *ch, sh, x,* and *s*. The words *catch, dish,* and *box* are made plural with *–es*. Irregular plurals are words that become plural in another way. For example, *child* becomes *children* and *die* becomes *dice*.

"Of course!" Ellen exclaimed with sudden understanding.

"What is it?" Kirk asked.

"I just figured out why E-s is the lead singer for 'Don't You Wish You Were a Rich Fox with a Dress Like Mine?' *Wish, rich, fox,* and *dress* are all words that she can make plural!"

"And what great things to have more of!" Kirk agreed.

"Except foxes maybe," Luke added. Kirk and Ellen gave each other a look and shook their heads.

"We have to tell Father what's going on." Kirk urged his siblings to come with him.

They found him in the sunroom again talking with the queen. He shared the startling news that E-s had confessed to kidnapping her sister S. But she refused to tell the police where she was.

Kirk related to the king the equally upsetting news about what was happening in Noun Town.

"For now, you're going to have to ask the guardians to make words plural. We have to get E-s to tell us where she is keeping her sister," the king said.

The three English children weren't surprised. They had already been discussing a mission entitled "Singular and Plural Nouns." They finalized it and sent it to the guardians right away.

What does *contrite* mean?

What is the singing group that Ellen was so excited to see?

What is a singular noun?

Chapter 23

It was board game night and Ellen was especially excited. The king and queen wanted something to take the place of video games. The queen suggested board games.

Although the king wasn't wildly enthusiastic, he **consented** — especially when the queen mentioned having special snacks.

★ ★ ★ ★ ★ ★ ★ ★ ★ ★

consented – *agreed*

★ ★ ★ ★ ★ ★ ★ ★ ★ ★

Each family member took turns choosing the games for the evening and it was Ellen's turn. She chose Apples to Apples ® because there was always a lot of laughter when they played it.

The family gathered in the game room. Comet found a comfy spot on the couch to watch. Ellen voted for the best example of something funny. The red apple cards the rest of the family turned in were funny, but not because they were supposed to be. When Ellen chose her father's card as the winner, Luke protested. "Ellen knew the card was Father's!"

"Luke, Ellen didn't know the card was Father's," Ellen said.

"Ellen did too! Ellen just didn't want to choose Luke's," Luke argued.

"Ellen and Luke are talking funny," Kirk chuckled.

"Yes, Ellen and Luke *are* talking funny," the queen agreed.

"Alright, let Mother, Kirk, Luke, and Ellen and the king try it again," the king suggested.

Kirk shrugged his shoulders and drew another card. This time the green apple card read *strange*. His family seemed to have trouble choosing red apple cards for this one. After reviewing them, Kirk chose Ellen's.

"Father, Mother, Kirk, Ellen, see!" Luke protested again. "Kirk and Ellen always choose Father or Ellen and not Luke."

"Luke, is Luke feeling okay?" Mother asked.

"Mother always thinks Luke is sick," Luke said.

"Definitely strange," Kirk said.

"Ellen's card was not strange. Luke's card was," Luke insisted.

"No, Luke. Kirk means the way Kirk, Ellen, Mother, Father, and Luke are talking is strange," Kirk said.

Ellen seemed near tears. "Tonight is Ellen's turn to choose the game and the whole night is ruined."

The king had a very tender heart where Ellen was concerned and sought to **console** her immediately. "Okay, okay, dear. Kirk, Luke, Mother, and the king will play the game with Ellen, won't Kirk, Luke, Mother, and the king?"

★ ★ ★ ★ ★ ★ ★ ★ ★ ★

console – *comfort*

★ ★ ★ ★ ★ ★ ★ ★ ★ ★

Ellen seemed distracted from her upset. "Kirk, Luke, Mother, and Father are talking strangely and Ellen is also!"

"Strange, alright," the king had to agree.

"Father, does Father think this is the Gremlin's doing?" Kirk asked.

"The king is concerned," he said.

"Father, do you think Father could help Kirk, Luke, and Ellen fix the problem? Then Kirk, Luke, Father, Mother, and Ellen can get back to playing the game sooner," Ellen pleaded.

"Well, Father doesn't have other activities planned. So Father will help Kirk, Luke, and Ellen," the king said. The three English children smiled in relief to have their father's help.

"Screen," the king commanded. "Give the king a galaxy status report, please."

"Certainly, Majesty," Screen replied. A series of news stories appeared and were dismissed as soon as the king said they weren't what he was looking for. Nothing appeared out of order.

"Now what do Kirk, Luke, Ellen, Mother, and Father do?" Kirk asked.

"The king, queen, Kirk, Luke, and Ellen will think about the differences in our speech," the king said.

"Luke knows!" Luke exclaimed.

"Yes, Luke, explain," the king answered.

"The king, queen, Kirk, Ellen, and Luke keep saying the names given to us," he said proudly. The king looked thoughtful.

"The meaning is?" Kirk asked his father.

★ ★ ★ ★ ★ ★ ★ ★ ★ ★

accommodations – *housing*

★ ★ ★ ★ ★ ★ ★ ★ ★ ★

"A specific part of speech is used to prevent the repetition of names. That specific part of speech seems to be missing," the king explained.

"The name of the part of speech is?" Ellen asked.

"Pronoun," said the king. "Screen, search any communication about pronouns, please." Screen responded and provided the king with a single letter.

Dear esteemed pronouns,

Congratulations on turning pro! Now that you have made the decision to be professional nouns, it's time to upgrade your **accommodations**. You don't have to live among the other nouns anymore.

We invite you to live in the prestigious gated community of Confinement Condominiums. Transportation will be provided for you using the enclosed tickets.

Imagine the lifestyle you can enjoy now that you've turned pro. No more repetitive word usage for you!
Enjoy a unique life sentence designed just for you. Everything is included at Confinement Condominiums.
You can be sure that the entire galaxy will appreciate you more once you start living like a true pro.

Sincerely,
The Committee for a Better Galaxy

"The Gremlin wrote this, didn't the Gremlin?" Luke asked.

"The king believes so, yes," the king said.

"Please explain, Father," Ellen said.

"The king suspects that many pronouns went to Confinement Condominiums after receiving the letter," the king said. "But the king doesn't think the pronouns are really in condominiums. Screen, can you give the king a view of the condos?"

After a few moments, the royal family could see what appeared to be a prison. The sign outside read "Confinement Condominiums." A high, barbed-wire fence surrounded the complex and the buildings' windows were barred shut.

"The pronouns aren't living with the rest of the nouns and they can't leave. So the king, queen, Luke, Ellen, and Kirk, and most likely other citizens of the planet can't say the words. Is Kirk correct?" Kirk asked.

The king nodded as he was beginning to become weary of speaking without pronouns.

"Do Kirk, Luke, and Ellen have to go to planet Sentence to release the pronouns, Father?" Ellen asked.

The king shook his head. "The king can send Grammar Patrol to let the pronouns out. But unlocking the doors won't necessarily solve the problem."

"Explain please, Father," Kirk urged.

"If the king knows the Gremlin, the conditions in that prison aren't bad. The Gremlin will make the words feel like royalty. The pronouns may not want to leave."

"Then Kirk, Luke, and Ellen should do...?" Kirk asked.

"The goal is to make the pronouns want to leave, right?" the king asked them. The children nodded. "Okay, then Kirk, Luke, and Ellen have to give the words the same treatment the words are receiving at the condominium."

"Ellen doesn't understand," she said. Her brothers indicated that they didn't either.

"Get the words to realize that the words can be treated like celebrities at home with the other nouns," the king suggested.

Ellen thought about it for a minute. "The king means the pronouns want fans?" He smiled his approval of her idea.

"Does Ellen have an idea?" Luke asked.

She nodded. "Ellen needs the guidebook."

The three English siblings headed to the library where they read an entry on pronouns.

Pronouns
Pronouns are nouns that take the place of other nouns so talking and writing are not as repetitive. There are several kinds of pronouns with personal pronouns being most common. Personal pronouns refer to people or things and include: *I, you, he, she, it, we, they, me, him, her, us,* and *them*. Note that the pronoun *I* is always capitalized.

"Kirk, Luke, and Ellen need to go to planet Sentence right away. Ellen can't take talking without the pronouns much longer!" Ellen complained. The boys agreed.

Kirk asked Ellen how she planned to make the pronouns feel like celebrities if they returned to Noun Town.

"Don't Kirk and Luke remember how S got back on tour? The guardians wrote fan letters, remember?" The boys smiled and nodded. "No trip to planet Sentence until the letters are written," she explained.

The three of them sent out a mission called "Pronouns" which they hoped would have them speaking normally before they were completely worn out.

What does *console* mean?

Was it confusing when the English family wasn't using pronouns?

What are the personal pronouns?

Chapter 24

It was Saturday morning and the king was reading his paper in the sunroom with the rest of the family. He had an announcement to make.

"The paper says it's going to be an beautiful day. I think we should take an hike." The family just stared at him.

"What's the matter? You don't want to go for an hike?"

"We would love to, dear," the queen said, patting him on the forearm.

"Wonderful. Let's get ready. Each of you get an water bottle and an snack to take with you." The children didn't move. "Get going! We don't want to waste the day, do we?" the king urged them. Comet barked as if to say he liked the plan.

"No, Father," Ellen answered, leading the way to the kitchen. When her brothers followed her in, she said, "Is Father talking funny?" Both boys agreed. "I hope he's okay!"

"I'm sure he's fine, El," Kirk said.

The family gathered with Comet at the back entrance to the palace. The king said, "I'll ask an servant to carry an backpack for us."

Kirk and Ellen traded glances. "Father, I'll be happy to carry the backpack. I could use the exercise," Kirk offered.

"That's an boy," the king said, smiling.

The three children got ahead of their parents on the hiking trail behind the castle. "I still notice it," Ellen said softly.

"Me too!" Luke said a bit more loudly.

"I do too," Kirk sighed. "Father is getting older." The three walked on **glumly** toward the stream that ran through the woods.

"An turtle!" Luke cried, pointing at the creature sunning itself on a log.

★ ★ ★ ★ ★ ★ ★ ★ ★ ★

glumly – unhappily

★ ★ ★ ★ ★ ★ ★ ★ ★ ★

"You mean an turtle," Kirk corrected. Luke ignored Kirk, jumping up and down and screeching in the hopes the turtle would dive in and swim. It didn't.

"I need an stick to scare him," Luke said, looking around for a large branch.

"Leave the poor turtle alone, Luke," Ellen urged, but Luke ignored her too. He finally chose a branch and slapped it against the water repeatedly. But the turtle remained motionless.

"I need an net," Luke said, dropping the stick, and running back to his parents. "Mother, Father, may I go back and get an net?"

"Annette, who is she?" the king asked.

"No, an net. You know for pulling fish out of the water. I want to catch an turtle."

"Aunt Urtle? You don't have an aunt by that name. Are you feeling alright?" he asked. The queen took the king's cue and felt Luke's forehead to see if he was feverish. When she nodded that he was fine, Kirk and Ellen joined them.

"Father, I think we have an problem," Kirk said.

"Anne Problem? Who is she? Luke has been talking about Annette and Aunt Urtle and now you're talking about Anne Problem. I just wanted to take an relaxing hike with my family," the king said impatiently.

"You wanted to take Anne on the hike? Why didn't you say so?" the queen asked him.

"I don't even know who Anne is!" the king roared.

"Father, if I may, I think we are having an grammar problem," Kirk said to calm his father.

"Who is Anne Grammar and what is her problem?" the queen asked.

"I don't think there's an Anne. We just keep saying it," Kirk explained further.

"We keep saying what?" the king asked.

"An," Kirk answered.

"But you said there isn't an Anne," the king said, getting **agitated**.

"There isn't an Anne that's the problem. We keep saying *an* before words and it sounds funny, like *an*

★ ★ ★ ★ ★ ★ ★ ★ ★ ★

agitated – tense

★ ★ ★ ★ ★ ★ ★ ★ ★ ★

turtle." The king was about to interrupt when Kirk continued. "Not Aunt Urtle, *an* turtle. You see?"

The king stroked his beard thoughtfully. "Now that you mention it, that does sound funny. Aunt Urtle. Of all the names!" he laughed.

Kirk sighed. "Father, I'm afraid we need to return to the castle. I suspect that the Gremlin has been at it again."

The king seemed disappointed until the queen said, "It's alright, dear. We haven't gone for an walk through the woods alone together in ages."

"You're quite right. Kirk, I trust you to solve our Anne problem. I expect a full report when we return."

"Certainly, Father! Luke, Ellen, let's head back. We have an mystery to solve."

The three English children made their way back to the castle without Comet, whose favorite thing next to table scraps was hiking. Luke returned very reluctantly. "Who cares if we say *an* a lot?" he complained.

"It sounds terrible," Ellen corrected him.

Kirk insisted that the three head directly to the library where he asked Screen for a status report. Everything seemed normal in the galaxy, which was surprising. "Have there been any events on any of the planets?" he asked. Nothing seemed noteworthy until Screen showed them a video of the Miss Article contest that was held on planet Sentence.

A reporter in a formal gown was standing in a theater with the crowned word *an* on the stage behind her. Words were mobbing *an*, trying to have their photo taken with her. "As you know, *the* dropped out of the contest, citing personal reasons," the reporter said. "That left *a* and *an* vying for the title of Miss Article. It had to be a tough choice for the judges. Oh wait! Here's one of the judges now," she added. She stopped a gentleman who seemed to be trying to leave the theater in a hurry. "What was the deciding factor for you in your vote for *an*?"

The man looked nervously around. "I can't say."

"Can you at least tell us what you were looking for in the contestants?"

"No, really. I can't say!" he said, brushing past the reporter.

"Okay! They must have rules about these things. Sorry, folks. As you can see behind me, the other words in the theater can't wait to get next to the newly crowned Miss Article—oh! I see *a*. Let's see if we can get a word. *A*! *A*! May we talk with you?" *A* seemed very discouraged.

"*A*, it must be disappointing, but it was such a close competition. Will you compete again next year?"

A said nothing but walked slowly away.

"As you can see, *a* is going to need some time before she can make a decision about next year. But for now, *an* is having the time of her life!"

"How many Miss Article competitions have there been?" Luke asked.

"I've never heard of it before," Ellen answered.

When the three asked Screen to search, their suspicion that this was the first competition was confirmed. Kirk started pacing.

"What is it, Kirk?" Ellen asked.

"This contest has to be behind our *an* problem. It's no **coincidence** that we keep saying *an*. Ellen, can you look up articles in the guidebook?"

★ ★ ★ ★ ★ ★ ★ ★ ★ ★

coincidence – *accident*

★ ★ ★ ★ ★ ★ ★ ★ ★ ★

"Sure." Ellen found two entries on articles, but only one included information on the word *an*.

Articles
Articles are adjectives. There are just three articles: *the*, *a*, and *an*. While *the* may be used with any word, *a* may only be used when the next word begins with a consonant sound. *An* may only be used when the next word begins with a vowel sound.

"The article *a* is upset because she lost the competition and all the words are clamoring to hang out with *an*. Is that what's making us say *an* for everything?" Ellen asked Kirk.

126

"That's my guess."

"Well, I'm guessing that the Gremlin got to the judges of this contest. Did you see how guilty that judge looked?" asked Ellen. Her brothers nodded. "So what do we do?"

"I think we head to planet Sentence!" Luke said, cheering up at the idea.

"Exactly what I was thinking!" Kirk said, giving Luke a high five. "We're going to have the contest declared a tie and crown *a* too."

"What about all of *an*'s fans? Many of those words should be fans of *a*, right?" Ellen said worriedly.

"That's true. When we get to planet Sentence and have *a* crowned an winner as well—whoops! There I go again. We'll invite all the words who should be with *a* to an exclusive party," Kirk said, proud of his own idea.

"I love it. But there were an lot of words there. How will we know which words should be invited?" Ellen asked.

"Couldn't the guardians help us?" Luke asked, eager to get going.

Kirk and Ellen smiled at each other. "He's really getting the hang of this," Kirk said.

When the three arrived at the theater, they used their communicators to snap photos of the words surrounding *an*. They asked Screen to send out a mission to their fellow guardians entitled "Articles."

What does *agitated* mean?

What was wrong with what the king said? *"I think we should take an hike."*

What three words are articles?

Chapter 25

Luke spent the afternoon at the main library branch doing his school assignments. He planned to reward himself with some video game time when he was done. And he hoped he could talk Kirk into playing with him for a while.

He was so excited that he was halfway home before he realized that he had left his communicator in the library. There were many signs in the library that reminded him to silence his communicator. So he had **complied** and had forgotten to put it back in his pocket.

Sighing, he headed back to the library. He wasn't happy when he

★ ★ ★ ★ ★ ★ ★ ★ ★ ★

complied – *obeyed*

★ ★ ★ ★ ★ ★ ★ ★ ★ ★

noticed that it wasn't where he had left it. Approaching the circulation desk, he said, "Excuse me" to the head librarian seated there. "I just left my communicator here. Would it be in Lost and Found?"

The librarian said, "Ah yes, someone just turned one in. Can you describe it for me?"

"Sure," Luke said. "It's—, well it's—, you know," he stammered while trying to show her with his hands.

"Yes? What kind is it?" the librarian encouraged him to continue.

"It's—. Hm," Luke thought aloud.

"Okay, what color is it?"

"Oh, that's easy. It's—, it's—. Ugh! I can't seem to describe it. It's just a communicator! Can I please have it?" he asked, getting frustrated.

"I see. Unfortunately, it is library policy not to give out missing items without a matching description. You understand. We want to make sure they are returned to their rightful owners."

"But I *am* the rightful owner!" Luke cried.

"Okay. Can you tell me how many buttons it has on the right?"

"Sure! It has—, it has—. I can't say!"

"Then I'm afraid I can't give it to you," the librarian said.

"Didn't you see me with it before?" Luke asked desperately.

"I'm afraid not. I just got here. I'm sorry."

Luke couldn't believe what had just happened as he made his way home. "Why couldn't she just give it to me?" he mumbled to himself. "And why couldn't I describe it?" The more he thought about what had happened, the faster he walked. He ended up running home.

He ran through the kitchen, completely ignoring Cook's offer of a snack. He finally found his father in the gym, lifting weights. "Hello, Luke! Would you like to join me for a workout?" the king asked.

Luke was so breathless, he had trouble speaking. "No...not now...I...was just...at the...library."

"It sounds like you've been running. Did they have an exercise class at the library? Seems a bit unusual."

"No...I...was doing school work," he answered, beginning to get his breath back.

"Wonderful! I'm so proud of you, Luke!" the king said patting him on the back. "But now I need to get back to my workout. I have gained a few pounds, believe it or not," he grinned, patting his belly.

"Father, about the library..." Luke said.

"Yes?"

Luke didn't want his father to lose his temper in the middle of a workout. "I will talk to you about it later."

"Sounds good," the king said.

Luke had an idea as he was leaving the gym. He could get Kirk to go to the library and describe his communicator and get it back for him. He knew what it looked like because his was the same style. He found his brother in the computer lab. When he explained what happened and what he wanted Kirk to do, Kirk groaned. He wasn't in the mood to interrupt his work. "Why can't you just describe it to her and get it back?" he asked.

"I don't know! Maybe she makes me nervous."

"Alright, I'll do it, but you owe me a favor."

Luke agreed and thanked his brother for helping him.

When Kirk arrived at the library, the head librarian was still at the circulation desk. "Hi," he said, trying to be as friendly as possible. "I left my communicator here and I was hoping it would be in Lost and Found."

"Oh sure," the librarian said. "Can you describe it for me?"

"Absolutely. It's—, it's like—." He used his hands to show her until he had an idea. "It's just like this one," he said, retrieving the communicator from his belt.

"I see," the librarian said suspiciously. "I thought you said you left your communicator here."

"Uh, well, actually. Okay, my brother lost his communicator here and he couldn't describe it and get it back," Kirk said in a rush.

"I remember."

"Oh good. Can I please have it? I'll return it right to him."

"No."

"No?" Kirk repeated, shocked.

"No. It's library policy. Didn't your brother tell you?"

"Yes, he mentioned it," Kirk said, reddening.

"Then why are you here?"

"I have no idea," Kirk said, leaving in a huff.

Kirk explained what had happened when he got back. Luke asked, "Why didn't you just describe it instead of showing her your communicator?"

"I tried! I couldn't!"

"Were you nervous too?" Luke asked.

Kirk didn't respond and they both sat thinking until their eyes met in alarm. The two of them left in a hurry to find their father enjoying a smoothie in the sunroom. "Boys, you ought to have a smoothie. It keeps your energy up!" the king suggested when he saw them.

"Maybe later," Kirk answered. "We have a problem."

"What now?" their father asked, putting his drink down to listen.

After the two boys explained what had happened in the library, they weren't surprised that their father seemed angry. They were hoping he would let the librarian have it.

"Kirk, you shouldn't have lied to the librarian," he said. "You will have to apologize."

Kirk was surprised but nodded. "You're right. I'm sorry, Father."

The king led the two boys into the adjacent dining room. "Screen, get me the head librarian, please," he commanded.

Soon she appeared on the screen. "Yes, Your Majesty. How may I be of service today?"

"First, my son Kirk has something to say."

"Uh, yes, I wanted to apologize for not being entirely truthful." When the king glared at him, he continued. "I mean I want to apologize for lying about the communicator. I should have told you the truth."

The librarian smiled. "All is forgiven. I do thank you for the apology, though."

Kirk smiled back and allowed his father to **resume** the conversation.

"Now then. I will send Luke over to pick up his communicator, alright?" the king asked.

★ ★ ★ ★ ★ ★ ★ ★ ★ ★

resume – *continue*

★ ★ ★ ★ ★ ★ ★ ★ ★ ★

"Absolutely! As soon as he describes it, he can have it," she said.

"Can he describe it now?" the king asked.

"I don't see why not."

"Okay, Luke, describe it for her, please."

"Well, remember I mentioned that I was having trouble with that? And so was Kirk?"

"A description please, Luke," the king said, smiling nervously at the librarian. "Tell her what kind it is, its color, how many buttons it has on the side, anything!"

"Uh, it is—. It's—." Luke was moving his hands frantically until he finally hung his head in shame. "I can't do it."

"Okay," the king said. "We'll get back to you," he told the librarian, ending the conversation.

"I believe you," he told the boys. "I've never known Luke to be at a loss for words. There's clearly a problem in the galaxy, but I'm going to leave it to you to solve it. I need a nap," he said, leaving the room.

Kirk wasted no time. "Screen, status report, please. Do there happen to be any words missing on planet Sentence?"

"There are no adjectives in Adjective Alley, Your Highness," Screen reported after a few moments.

"Where are they?" Kirk asked.

"Their whereabouts are unknown. Here is a copy of a party invitation sent to all adjectives."

You are invited to the most amazing, fabulous, and fun party ever! Come to 12345 Blue Avn., **Vague** Way.

"Screen, can you get me a view of the party location?" Kirk asked.

In a few seconds, Screen reported, "Your Highness, there is no such address."

★ ★ ★ ★ ★ ★ ★ ★ ★ ★

vague – *unclear*

★ ★ ★ ★ ★ ★ ★ ★ ★ ★

"Kirk, what is Avn.? Is that supposed to be A-v-e-period for Avenue?" Luke asked.

"Probably. Is there a Blue Avenue in Vague Way?" Kirk asked Screen.

"I'm afraid there is no Vague Way in my records," Screen responded.

"The adjectives are lost," Kirk realized, speaking aloud. "Luke, go get Ellen and tell her we have to head to planet Sentence to find them."

"Okay, but Kirk, what's an adjective?" Luke asked, embarrassed.

The two boys found their sister and headed to the castle library to look up adjectives in the guidebook.

Adjectives
Adjectives are words that describe nouns and answer the questions *what kind*, *which one*, and *how many*. They describe color, size, shape, number, appearance, speed, taste, touch, personality, and more.

"Wow! No wonder I couldn't describe my communicator," Luke exclaimed.

"Yes, and your lost communicator is the least of our worries if we can't find the adjectives," Kirk added.

The three decided to send out an emergency mission on identifying adjectives before they left to locate them.

What does *vague* mean?

Why couldn't Luke describe his communicator?

What adjectives were used to describe the party in the party invitation?

Chapter 26

"What should we do this weekend?" the king asked when they were having breakfast one Saturday morning. Comet lay sleeping under the dining table.

Ellen let out a long sigh. "I don't know."

The king frowned. "Do you have any ideas, Luke?"

"Not really," Luke said, staring at his plate.

The king was getting **perturbed**. "Kirk, what about you? You're always up for something fun."

★ ★ ★ ★ ★ ★ ★ ★ ★ ★

perturbed – *annoyed*

★ ★ ★ ★ ★ ★ ★ ★ ★ ★

"Yeah, usually I am. But I just don't feel like doing anything," Kirk said apologetically.

"Dear, what is wrong with our children? We have two beautiful days to do some active things as a family. And I'm getting no enthusiasm here," he complained.

The queen sat staring at her plate too. "Hm. I don't know, dear," she said with seeming great effort.

"Are you all ill?" the king asked with rising irritation.

The rest of the family shook their heads no.

"Well then, we aren't just going to sit around all day! Let's get ready to go somewhere. How about a trip and a picnic to Galaxy Gardens? We could use the paddle boats and feed the ducks. We've always enjoyed that," he said.

The queen and the children sat slumped in their seats but tried to fake enthusiasm. "Yeah, sure," they murmured.

The king clapped his hands and ordered them to get busy preparing for the trip. He also requested that the kitchen staff prepare a tasty picnic lunch. But the staff were slow to respond as well. "We are leaving in half an hour," the king warned them, thinking that they would move faster. But they leaned against the counters, looking as though they were about to fall asleep. When he repeated himself in a much louder voice, they started working.

134

Normally Comet would be wagging his tail, eager to go with them. But he continued sleeping soundly. The king had his hands full trying to get his family ready, so he decided to leave him behind.

The king was quite irritated by the time lunch was ready and his family members were in the royal carriage. He didn't understand what was wrong with everyone, but he hoped that the fresh air would perk them up.

He pointed out anything he could find on the way to spark their enthusiasm—wild animals, lovely homes, and unusual cloud shapes. But his family continued to seem bored.

When they arrived at the gardens, he had to coax them out of the carriage. Whenever he wasn't looking, the kids or queen would sit on a bench, and he would have to go back for them. He was running out of patience and motivators.

When they weren't even interested in the **delectable** lunch that had been prepared, he knew something was wrong.

★ ★ ★ ★ ★ ★ ★ ★ ★ ★

delectable – *delicious*

★ ★ ★ ★ ★ ★ ★ ★ ★ ★

"Have you been staying up late?" he asked. "You don't have any energy!"

Everyone reluctantly admitted that they had.

"I've been reading a book I just can't put down," Ellen said.

"And I've been creating a really cool computer game," Kirk added.

"Once I start watching funny videos, I have a hard time stopping," Luke explained.

"I feel like that about home decorating websites," the queen agreed. "I should have gone to bed earlier."

"Well, that settles it!" the king declared. "We are all going to get to sleep earlier so we can enjoy our weekend. Look at this!" the king said, pointing to the lake. "It's too lovely to miss."

The rest of the family nodded their agreement, but the rest of the outing continued in the same way. Everyone but the king seemed content to just sit and stare.

On the way home, the king muttered, "I went to bed at a reasonable hour. I have all the energy I need. It's ridiculous to be so sleepy when there is so much to do." The queen and the children said nothing.

The next morning after an early bedtime, the queen and the kids seemed just as sluggish as they were the day before. Comet didn't seem to have moved from his sleeping spot. But this time the king did not complain, because he was in the same **stupor**.

★ ★ ★ ★ ★ ★ ★ ★ ★ ★

stupor – *daze*

★ ★ ★ ★ ★ ★ ★ ★ ★ ★

Breakfast was very slow to be served and no one seemed to care. They sat staring without eating, sighing occasionally. Screen interrupted the quiet. "Excuse me, Your Majesty, but there is something I must bring to your attention."

Normally, the king would give Screen permission to speak and the report would proceed. This time, the king just stared ahead, so after a long pause, Screen continued. "Your Majesty, there is a matter of importance on planet Sentence for you to attend to." When there was still no response from the king, Screen said, "It could explain why you aren't feeling like yourself."

That statement seemed to get through to the king because he mumbled, "Go on."

"The Action Film Festival is going on in Verb Village."

"That sounds fun," Kirk sighed.

"Yes," Screen answered. "Most of the verbs in the village and a number of other words on the planet are attending."

"Are they showing any good action films this year?" Luke asked, yawning.

"No, they're not, Your Highness," Screen answered. "These are films that have no action. That's the problem. See what's happening," he directed, opening a live video feed. The camera focused on the film playing on the movie screen. It featured a boy sleeping in a darkened room. The English family watched, waiting for something to happen, but the scene didn't change. The boy kept sleeping. The camera angle of the video feed changed to show thousands of words seated in the dark theater. Most of their eyes were closed.

"They're sleeping," Ellen said with apparent envy.

"Correct, Your Highness. That means most of the galaxy's verbs are sleeping."

The king sat up straight with great effort. "This is a disaster," he said quietly. "And it explains why we have no energy. Kirk, the guardians have to do something." He insisted that the three children

136

go to the library and look up verbs in the guidebook. It took them a long time to get there, but they were glad they had come when they read the entry.

Verbs
A verb is a word that expresses action or a state of being. Action verbs include *go, walk, jump,* and *eat*. They are things someone or something can do. Verbs that express states of being include *am, are, is, was,* and *were*.

"If all the verbs were sleeping, we wouldn't even exist, would we?" Ellen asked.

"Probably not," Kirk answered. "But I don't think every verb is sleeping."

"The action verbs are. They wanted to see action films, and the festival definitely isn't showing action films," Luke added.

"It explains why we are so tired and don't want to do anything. The action verbs aren't doing anything," Kirk said.

"Now what? I really just want a nap, but I'm guessing I won't be getting one," Ellen said.

"You guessed right, El. We have to go to the Film Festival in Verb Village," Kirk said. He explained to his brother and sister that if they showed a popular action movie at the festival, they could wake up the action verbs.

"But it will cost a lot of money to do that, won't it? And words that aren't action verbs will want to see it too!" Luke said, worrying aloud.

"You're right. We will have to limit admission to action verbs only in order to keep costs down." Kirk saw that Ellen had another worry and addressed it before she spoke. "And we'll need the guardians to help us identify who should get in to see the movie."

The three of them created a mission called "Verbs." They sent it out before they left for planet Sentence.

What is a *stupor*?

Why didn't the English family have any energy?

What is an action verb?

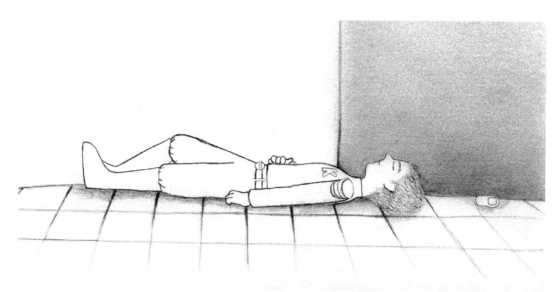

Chapter 27

Kirk was sneaking to his bedchamber, hoping he could avoid being caught. Despite his father's order that he be in bed early, he had continued working late on his computer program. As he passed by the castle art gallery, he saw a shadow move, so he stopped to see if he had just been seeing things.

When he had held still—holding his breath even—and nothing had moved for what felt like minutes, Kirk decided to turn on the lights. He wanted to be sure. Rather than try to reach a switch, he turned on the gallery lights using his communicator. He was startled when he saw a man dressed in black running toward him with a painting in his arms.

"Stop!" Kirk commanded, trying to block the thief's getaway. But the man didn't even slow down, knocking Kirk from his feet. Kirk's head hit the marble floor with a *thwack* and his communicator flew out of his grasp.

When Kirk awoke, he was in the castle infirmary. His mother was leaning over his bed, staring anxiously at his face. When she saw that he was waking, she called for the doctor to come quickly.

The royal physician was an elderly, **bespectacled** man who rarely had to call on the family. He did his best to calm the queen and greeted Kirk warmly. "You've got quite a bump on the back of your head!" he said, examining Kirk's eyes. "Let's see if everything looks okay."

★ ★ ★ ★ ★ ★ ★ ★ ★ ★

bespectacled – *glasses-wearing*

observation – *watching*

grimacing – *frowning*

★ ★ ★ ★ ★ ★ ★ ★ ★ ★

With the comment on his head, Kirk began to feel the pain of his fall and groaned. Suddenly he remembered. "He took the painting!" he cried, trying to sit up.

"Easy, easy there, Kirk," the doctor said, pushing him gently back against the pillows. "We'll get to that. Let's just make sure you're okay."

After the doctor examined him thoroughly, he told his parents, "I've looked at his brain scan. I think he should stay overnight for **observation**."

Kirk groaned again. "Okay, but we need to catch the guy who stole our painting. I need to talk to a detective," he said, **grimacing** in pain.

When the doctor left, the rest of the family came in to see Kirk. They were relieved to see him awake and talking normally. He kept insisting that they call in a detective, so his father gave in and made the call. When he was finished, he said, "Kirk, the painting doesn't matter. I'm just so glad you're okay."

"I should have stopped him!" Kirk said, pounding his fist on the bed.

"Don't be silly! Your father is right. We're just glad you're safe," his mother said, patting his hand.

Kirk seemed comforted some time later when the detective knocked on his door. "Hello! I understand a crime has been committed?" he asked as he came in.

The king and queen nodded and shooed Luke and Ellen out of the room. That made room for the detective to sit down and talk to Kirk undisturbed.

The detective nervously pulled out a notebook and pen to take notes. "I'm old school," he admitted.

When the king and queen smiled their approval, the detective addressed Kirk. "Okay, let's get started. Can you describe the man who was taking the painting?"

"Sure," Kirk said eagerly. "He was tall and muscular and dressed in black. He wore a black mask too, so I couldn't see his face."

The detective wrote this down. "Okay, got it. That's very helpful. Now when was this?"

Kirk thought for a moment. "It was dark."

"Uh-huh, so when did it happen approximately?"

Kirk sat up straight, seeming to search for words. "It was dark," he said wearily, letting his shoulders fall back against the pillows.

"Right. You said that. Just tell me where you were when you saw him."

Kirk squinted with effort and moaned in defeat. "It was dark."

The detective caught the queen's eye to communicate that he thought something was wrong. "Kirk," he said, "would you excuse us a minute?" Kirk nodded and the three adults went out into the hallway to talk.

"What exactly did the doctor say about Kirk's condition?" the detective asked.

"He said he hit his head pretty hard," the queen answered, looking worried.

"I see. That would explain why he can't remember what happened."

"The doctor didn't tell us he would have memory loss," the king said.

"It's normal; don't worry. Let's give him a good night's rest and I will come back to talk with him tomorrow. In the meantime, I will talk to your night staff in case they saw anything."

The king and queen agreed with the detective's plan and thanked him for his help.

The next morning, the detective came to visit Kirk again. This time, Kirk was all smiles. "I think someone is feeling better," the detective said.

"Definitely!" Kirk agreed.

"Perfect. Are you ready to answer a few more questions?" he asked, retrieving his notebook.

"Yes!"

"Okay, Kirk, you said it was dark when you saw the thief with the painting. Do you remember when you saw him?"

Kirk's smile faded as he realized he didn't know.

The detective saw his upset. "Don't worry about it, buddy. Do you remember where you saw him?"

After some hesitation, Kirk shook his head, and seemed on the verge of tears. The detective put his notebook away and patted Kirk on the shoulder. "We'll catch him, Kirk. Don't worry."

The detective spoke to the king and queen in the hallway again. "This memory loss doesn't seem normal," the queen said. "We need to call the doctor!" The detective agreed and the queen left to call him.

"Did my staff give you any information?" the king asked. "Did they see anything?"

"I'm afraid not. I did speak with your night watchman who said he saw a suspicious-looking man. He described him the same way Kirk did. But he couldn't tell me where he saw him, when he saw him, or how he thought he got the painting out of the castle."

"That's odd," the king said, stroking his beard. "If he saw the thief, why can't he tell you when and where he was?"

"My thoughts exactly."

"You think he did it, don't you?"

"Right now, he's our only lead."

The king suggested that the detective question the rest of his staff about the night watchman. He asked for a report when he was done.

Several hours later, the doctor pronounced Kirk well enough to return to his own bedchamber. He gave strict orders for him to rest, however.

The detective didn't have good news for the king when he met with him in his study. "I interviewed several of your staff members about the night watchman. They told me he is an honest, hard-working man and that they didn't think he would steal from you. But when I asked them when and where they had last seen him, they couldn't answer me."

"Do you think they were all in on it?" the king asked, shocked by the possibility.

"Anything's possible," the detective shrugged. "Do you mind if I ask you a few questions?"

"I'm happy to," the king agreed.

"Alright. When did you last see Kirk before the painting was taken?"

"Ummmm, I—, hm," the king stuttered.

The detective's eyes grew wide. "You can't remember?"

The king shook his head no.

"Okay, where did you last see him before the theft then?"

The king seemed deep in thought and then shrugged.

"I'm afraid I know what's going on here," the detective said.

"You do?" the king asked, amazed that he'd solved the crime so quickly.

"Yes, you had your own painting stolen."

"What?" the king yelled. "That's ridiculous!"

The two began arguing when Screen interrupted them. "Your Majesty, I have a progress report for you on the relocation of Adverb Village."

"What relocation?" the king asked. "I didn't order Adverb Village to be relocated."

Screen showed footage of Adverbs moving into tents in what appeared to be a desert.

"Adverbs have to live near Verbs!" the king exclaimed. "Excuse me, Detective. I have to handle this crisis and then we can get back to discussing the theft."

The detective agreed to come back later and the king alerted Luke and Ellen to the situation. Their first action was to find and read the entry on Adverbs in the guidebook.

Adverbs
An adverb is a word that tells how, when, or where. Adverbs often explain verbs and frequently end in *–ly*. The words *slowly*, *later*, and *nearby* are all adverbs.

"No wonder Kirk couldn't answer the detective's questions!" Ellen exclaimed. "The adverbs have been moved away from the verbs they explain."

"Right. So now what?" Luke asked.

"Now we have to get the adverbs back to the old location for Adverb Village."

"Ugh. Another word-relocation mission? And without Kirk?" Luke complained.

"Oh, come on, Luke. We have the guardians to help us. And going into the desert will be an adventure!"

Luke had to admit he loved adventure. He agreed to help Ellen create a mission called "Adverbs."

What does *observation* mean?

Why did the detective think the king had his own painting stolen?

What is an adverb?

Chapter 28

It was another Saturday morning and the English family was seated at the breakfast table. The king was cheerful. "Now that the verbs and adverbs are where they ought to be, we can enjoy a fun family outing to the zoo?" he asked.

The children squirmed. "Actually, I was going to ask you...I'm going out with friends today," Kirk said.

"You're going out with friends," the king said.

"Oh, thanks for understanding, Father," Kirk said, getting up to leave.

"But I didn't give you permission," the king said so quietly that Kirk didn't hear.

"Bye, everyone?" Kirk asked. Everyone but the king waved.

"Uh, I was going to ask too. I'm going to the ball game today with my friends!" Luke shouted.

"That's how you talk to me," the king said softly.

"Great," Luke muttered. "Thank you?" he asked.

The king threw up his arms in frustration. "We are going to spend time together as a family?" he asked.

"No!" the queen shouted. "I was going to ask you if I could have lunch with the ladies."

"You too," the king said.

"Thank you?" the queen asked, excusing herself.

"I guess it's just you and me, Ellen!" the king shouted.

"I have plans with friends too!" Ellen yelled back.

"You mean you're asking to go," the king whispered.

"Yes?" Ellen asked.

The king nodded and suddenly felt **fatigued**. "I'm going back to bed?" he asked himself, heading to his bedchamber.

★ ★ ★ ★ ★ ★ ★ ★ ★ ★

fatigued – *tired*

★ ★ ★ ★ ★ ★ ★ ★ ★ ★

After a nap, the king decided that he needed to talk with his family about respect. Everyone was telling him what they were going to do without asking permission. It was unusual and disappointing. The king had hoped they could go to the zoo together. But since everyone was gone, he realized it was a good opportunity to invite his friend to play golf.

He called Ernie on his communicator. "Ernie," the king said. "I called to ask...you're going to play golf with me!"

"I am," Ernie said, surprised.

"Wonderful?" the king asked.

"You are ordering me to play golf with you," Ernie said. "Because you're the king!"

"I am ordering you to play golf with me!" the king shouted, but he was really asking why Ernie thought he was ordering him.

"Unbelievable?" Ernie asked and then hung up.

The king thought Ernie had gotten disconnected and called again. "Ernie! So you're going to meet me at the course in half an hour!" he shouted.

Ernie replied, "You're serious," and hung up again.

"Everyone is crazy today?" the king asked himself.

The king was in a very foul mood by the time everyone returned home. He had tried to occupy himself with a book. He took Comet for a walk around the castle grounds. He lifted weights. But he was lonely.

"How was lunch!" he shouted at the queen when she greeted him with a kiss.

"Lovely?" she asked, smiling.

"You aren't sure," the king replied.

"I'm sure it was lovely!" the queen shouted.

"Okay?" the king asked, afraid to upset her further. He assumed it hadn't gone well and she didn't want to talk about it.

He had similar conversations with the children when they returned home.

At dinner that evening, he asked, "I'm very concerned about the lack of respect shown me?"

"You are!" the queen yelled.

146

"That's what I'm talking about?" asked the king.

The children watched their argument with great concern.

"What's wrong!" Kirk shouted.

Ellen stared at her communicator, astonished. "Every time I text something to my friend, it gets changed?" she asked.

"You're not supposed to be texting at dinner?" her father asked.

"What do you mean!" the queen shouted at Ellen.

"I mean that when I tell her something, it gets changed to a question or it looks like I'm yelling! She is getting mad at me?" she asked.

"Screen!" the king shouted. "Please advise," he added quietly.

A status report of the galaxy began scrolling across the screen. The king saw one report that interested him and touched it. A news report began to play.

"I am here on planet Sentence where a new beautification law has taken effect," a reporter said. "Too many signs take away from the view, **legislators** have decided. As a result, these signs have been removed and put into storage." The view changed to piles of stop signs. They had periods, question marks, and exclamation marks on them.

★ ★ ★ ★ ★ ★ ★ ★ ★ ★

legislators – *lawmakers*

petrified – *terrified*

★ ★ ★ ★ ★ ★ ★ ★ ★ ★

"Great grammar?" the king asked.

"What is it!" the queen shouted.

"We can't go on talking this way," the king whispered.

The queen looked **petrified**. "We can work it out?" she asked.

"Dear, this is a problem for the guardians to solve!" he yelled at the queen, taking her hand. "Kirk, Luke, Ellen, go to the library and look up end marks in the guidebook?" he asked, pointing at the door.

"We'll go?" Kirk asked, motioning for his siblings to follow. The conversation on the way became so confusing that the three children stopped speaking. They understood when Ellen read the entry for end marks.

End Marks
There are three end marks: the period, question mark, and exclamation point. All three punctuation marks indicate the end of a sentence. Periods are used at the end of statements or **declarative** sentences. Sentences that declare something usually end in periods. Question marks are at the end of questions. *Interrogate* means to question, so these sentences are called **interrogative** sentences. They often begin with *who, what, where, when, why* and *how*. Finally, exclamation marks come at the end of sentences that express strong emotion. These are called **exclamatory** sentences.

"All of our end marks have gotten mixed up?" Ellen asked, though she intended to make it a statement.

"Yes," Luke said, though he meant it as an exclamation.

The English siblings were able to communicate that they needed to head to planet Sentence. They planned to get all the end mark signs put back where they belonged.

"How will we know where they go!" Ellen shouted.

"That's a good question?" Kirk asked, though he meant it as a statement.

The three decided that they would need the guardians' help to sort the signs out. They hoped that the mission called "End Marks" would have them speaking normally and getting along again. After they wrote the mission, they prepared to use the space porter. They didn't want to risk long conversations in the shuttle that would only lead to confusion.

What are *legislators*?

Why was Ernie mad at the king?

What are the three end marks?

Chapter 29

"You made the front page of *The Grammar Gazette* again!" Luke exclaimed. He stood behind his father while he studied the newspaper after breakfast.

"Indeed!" the king said proudly.

"What's the article about this time?" Kirk asked.

"My biography. I spoke with a reporter about the changes that were made to it because—you know—it was a little exaggerated."

"You mean it was a tall tale," Ellen said giggling.

"The author just thought so highly of me after getting to know me," the king said, defending himself.

The three English children just smiled.

"Why don't you read the article to us, dear?" the queen asked sweetly.

The king was happy to do so.

"After a recall of the king's biography for factual errors, I had the chance to sit down with our beloved **monarch**. We talked about the revised book, which will soon be released. I asked him if what I had heard about the mistakes in the biography were true and he said they were. Based on his statements, we can assume that the king is not as strong, smart, and generous as his biographer wanted us to believe.

★ ★ ★ ★ ★ ★ ★ ★ ★ ★

monarch – *ruler*

fretfully – *worriedly*

cringed – *flinched*

★ ★ ★ ★ ★ ★ ★ ★ ★ ★

"I also asked the king about the recent theft of a very valuable painting from the castle art gallery. He said he didn't know anything about the crime. We can take from this that the king doesn't take this crime seriously. A biography full of lies and a crime cover-up is making citizens suspicious of this once trusted leader."

The king's face turned red as he thought about what he had just read.

"Dear, remember not to lose your temper," the queen said. She got up and **fretfully** patted him on the arm.

"This is terrible reporting!" the king yelled. The rest of the family **cringed**. "That is not what I said about the book! And about the painting...I didn't say I didn't know anything about it. I said the police don't have a suspect yet, but that we had cooperated fully. I just can't believe this!"

The queen did her best to calm him down, but the king paced as he thought aloud about what to do. "I'm going to get him fired! No, wait, if I do that, everyone will think what he wrote is true. I could take him to court for telling lies! But that would take so long and the damage is already done."

"I don't think anyone will believe what he wrote, dear," the queen said.

"This is going to ruin the book sales too!" the king said with a sudden realization.

"We don't know that, dear."

The king groaned and picked up the article again. "There aren't any direct quotes from me. I must have spent two hours with him. And all he wrote was that I said that the mistakes he heard about were true? And that I knew nothing about the crime? I told him in detail that my biographer was too kind in describing my strength, intelligence, and generosity. I said I wanted it to be rewritten. I said I didn't want people to think I was Superman. Is that written in here? No!"

"It's strange that he wouldn't have written that last part," Kirk said. "That's a good one. It would have made a good headline even."

"Well, he didn't use anything I said," the king said, throwing the paper down in disgust. "I need to take a break from the news and calm down," he said, excusing himself and leaving the room.

"Poor Father," Ellen said sadly. "Why did that reporter have to make him sound so bad?"

"I don't know," the queen said, hugging her daughter. "But we know how good your father really is." All three kids nodded.

Later that afternoon, Kirk searched online for reactions to the article about his father. He was relieved not to find anything negative. He did, however, find a news article that looked interesting. When he opened it, a video started. It showed two people painting a wall white while a narrator explained. "The Beautiful Planet Project is keeping these painters busy here on planet Sentence. They are removing graffiti from walls, bridges, and signs. Any writing or artwork in public places that was not put there legally will be painted over."

The scene on the video changed to painters covering up quotation marks on signs. "The biggest job will be removing this kind of graffiti because it is *everywhere*," the reporter said.

Kirk was concerned about the last part of the video and wanted to discuss it with his father. But when he looked for him, he found that he was taking a nap and Kirk didn't want to disturb him. When he went to look for his brother and sister, the butler told him that Luke was out playing catch with a friend. He said Ellen was practicing piano in the music room.

"How is it a problem to get rid of graffiti?" Ellen asked after Kirk found her and explained what he had seen.

"It's not really. It's how they are defining graffiti that is the problem. I think we need the guidebook."

"Why? Nothing is going wrong because they're cleaning up planet Sentence, right?"

"I'm not so sure of that. I wonder if there could be a connection between the graffiti clean-up and Father's article."

"Really? If we can do something to cheer him up, we should. Let's go."

When the two got to the library, Ellen immediately looked up graffiti in the guidebook. She didn't find an entry.

"Let's look it up in the dictionary," Kirk suggested.

Ellen found it on the page with the guide words *graceful* and *grand*. "It says it means writing or drawing put illegally in a public place. Does that help?"

"Yes. Now look up quotation marks in the guidebook."

Ellen read the entry to Kirk.

Quotation Marks

Quotation marks (") are punctuation usually used to show the exact words that someone said. They indicate a **direct quote**. For example: He said, "We don't know anything about it." A comma or end mark comes before a quote and the first word of a quote is capitalized. A comma or end mark also goes *inside* the last set of quotes. For example: "We don't know anything about it," he said. Quotation marks are not used for a summary of what someone said. For example: He said they didn't know anything about it. This type of report is called an **indirect quote**.

"Quotation marks could be considered graffiti on planet Sentence in public places, right?" Ellen asked.

"They're not illegal though," Kirk said. "They shouldn't be, anyway. Screen, can you give me the law there on quotation marks?"

Screen quickly produced the information and read it for Kirk. "Writing on signs in public places is illegal as part of the Beautiful Planet Project. The king recently ruled that the law does not apply to end mark signs."

"Uh-oh. We're going to have to change the law again," Kirk sighed. "The law should not apply to *any* punctuation. And this explains why the article about Father was so bad."

"How?"

"The writer used no quotes because he couldn't without the quotation marks. The readers don't know exactly what Father said."

"How do we fix it?"

"We need to demand a follow-up article with direct quotes. But first we have to put the quotation marks back where they belong."

"That will take forever," Ellen groaned.

"Not with the guardians' help," Kirk said smiling.

The two of them wrote a mission they called "Quotation Marks." They then went to find Luke and update him before their trip to planet Sentence.

What is a *monarch*?

Which kind of quote didn't the reporter use: direct or indirect?

What is graffiti?

Unit V: Adventures in Composition & Speaking

Chapter 30

The queen was walking past Luke's bedchamber late one night when she noticed his light was still on. She knocked quietly and opened the door when he answered.

"Why are you still up, young man?" she asked.

Luke was sitting up in bed writing in a workbook. He seemed upset. "This homework is taking forever!" he cried.

"Of course, it is. You can't do good work late at night. Get some sleep and you'll get it done when you're fresh tomorrow."

"But I'm so behind!"

"That's because you haven't been studying when you're supposed to be," the queen corrected him.

Luke sighed. He couldn't deny it. "Alright, I'll go to bed."

The queen kissed him good-night and headed to bed herself.

Just as the queen was falling asleep, she remembered something she wanted to tell the kitchen staff. She knew from experience that if she didn't write it down, she would forget. She grabbed a notepad and pen she kept by the bed and went near a nightlight to see. She didn't want to turn on a lamp and risk waking the king.

The queen began to write and noticed something strange. She felt like she was writing in a dream. Each letter seemed to take minutes to form. The process was so irritatingly slow that she couldn't remember what she wanted to write. She decided that she was just exhausted. The note wasn't that important anyway. She put the notepad and pen away and went to sleep.

The next morning the three English children attended a library field trip. An award-winning author would be teaching galaxy students how to write short stories. After she was introduced, the author asked them for the titles of their favorite books. She stood in front of a large white board and started writing as the children shared.

In just a few moments, however, the children stopped shouting out titles. They just **gaped** at the author, who was taking a full minute to form each letter on the white board. "I—, I—, don't know what's wrong with me," the author stammered. "I'm afraid I need a break."

★ ★ ★ ★ ★ ★ ★ ★ ★ ★

gaped – *stared*

administrator – *manager*

hastily – *hurriedly*

★ ★ ★ ★ ★ ★ ★ ★ ★ ★

The children murmured as she rushed out of the room. The man who had introduced her quieted them. "I'm sure she'll be back in a minute. In the meantime, why don't you all make a list of your favorite books to share with her?"

Some assistants passed out paper and pencils. The children became occupied with deciding on their favorites and writing them down. It wasn't long, however, before the murmuring began again. Kirk thought he knew what it was about. He was unable to write quickly too. Each letter seemed to take forever to form. It was like trying to write under water. He decided to approach the **administrator** and tell him what was happening.

The man was incredulous until Kirk suggested he try to write something on the white board. He **hastily** grabbed the marker and planned to prove that Kirk was being ridiculous. But he, too, found writing to be aggravatingly slow. He put the marker down as quickly as he had picked it up. "So what do we do?" he asked Kirk secretively.

"You could tell our guest speaker that all will be well if no one hand writes anything. She can still teach everyone how to write short stories. I am going to return home and see if I can learn something about why this is happening."

The administrator gratefully agreed. The program continued with the author looking greatly relieved as well. Kirk slipped out of the room without telling his siblings.

When Kirk arrived at the castle, he was met by his mother, who was surprised to find him home. After he explained what had happened, she told him about the note she had been unable to write the night before. Kirk excused himself to head to the library to research the problem. But the queen remembered something else. "And your brother! He said he couldn't finish his homework. Do you think it was the handwriting problem?"

"I do," Kirk agreed.

In the library, Kirk asked Screen for a status report. Nothing significant popped up for any of the planets, so Kirk asked for more details. "Tell me anything at all that is happening on planet Composition."

Screen soon produced a lot of information that Kirk scrolled through. "Road construction...," he said to himself. "Where is the road construction happening exactly?" he asked Screen.

"Handwriting City, Your Highness."

Kirk groaned. "Can you show me any pictures of the progress?" Soon pictures of road blocks and videos of construction workers filled the screen. They were using jack hammers on the roads in Handwriting City. "This is going to take forever," he grumbled. Kirk decided he had to let his father know what was happening.

The king was in his study holding his pen over a sheet of paper when Kirk knocked. When Kirk told him what was going on, the king was delighted. "I thought I had lost my ability to write! I have spent all morning trying to sign this document. Now I know why. Thank you, Kirk!"

"No problem, Father. But now what do we do?"

"I can send more workers to get the road construction finished faster. But I don't think that's the answer," the king said. When Kirk asked him why not, he continued. "Slow handwriting is a problem even without the road construction. We write things by hand less and less. Most of the time we type and we use our voice to dictate too. When we do write, we are slow."

"But do we really need to write by hand anymore?" Kirk asked.

"Yes, there is still a need for it. Many lessons are in paper format. There are paper forms to complete and sign. And writing by hand has been shown to improve spelling and memory. Students who can't write fast will often put off doing lessons because they take so long to finish."

"Are you saying we need to improve our handwriting speed?"

"That's what I'm saying," the king said. "The faster our students write, the faster the road construction in Handwriting City will be completed too."

"I have an idea. If I can put a handwriting mission together quickly, I can make it back to the library with it. I can give it to the guardians who are attending. We can start increasing our handwriting speed right away!"

"That's an excellent idea, Kirk."

What does *gaped* mean?

Why was everyone's handwriting so slow?

Why is it important to write faster?

Chapter 31

Luke headed to the main library branch, excited to pick up a new book he had reserved. It was the latest book in a series he was crazy about.

When he arrived, he asked the librarian where he would find it. She explained that it was located on a shelf, alphabetized by the last name of the person who had requested it. He found the E section and retrieved his prize gleefully. He didn't want to stay in the library to read—the day was too beautiful—so he took it to the scanner to check it out.

The first step in the checkout process was to scan his library card. When he did that, he received a message that he would have to see the librarian before checking out books. Luke was feeling a little frustrated but told himself it wouldn't take long.

"Excuse me," he said to the librarian. "I scanned my card and the screen said I had to see you."

"Oh yes, your library card has probably expired. Let me check." Luke **dutifully** handed over the card which she scanned. "Yes, that's the problem. I will just need you to complete a new form," she said, pulling out a sheet from underneath the counter. She put it on a clipboard with an attached pen and told Luke to complete it at one of the library tables.

★ ★ ★ ★ ★ ★ ★ ★ ★ ★

dutifully – *obediently*

envisioned – *imagined*

assistance – *help*

★ ★ ★ ★ ★ ★ ★ ★ ★ ★

Luke sighed and sat down hard at the table. This was not how he **envisioned** his day going. As he worked on the form, his annoyance grew. "Why do they need all this information just so I can check out a book?" he muttered. "I don't even know what some of this means." He decided to ask Kirk for **assistance**.

"Kirk," he said into his communicator. "What does gender mean?"

"It means male or female, why?"

"I'm at the library and they won't let me check out a book without filling out a form," he complained.

The librarian heard Luke and shushed him.

"Ugh. I can't talk now, Kirk," he said, hanging up.

Luke started writing his name at the top of the form before he realized he was supposed to write his last name first. He couldn't erase it because it was in pen. He approached the desk again. "Uh, excuse me? Sorry, but I wrote my first name where it says last name and I can't erase it. Could I have a new form?"

It was the librarian's turn to be annoyed. "Alright," she sighed. "Last name first this time."

"Got it!" Luke agreed, sitting down. He wrote English first and then Luke and was pleased to be finished with that part. Next, he wrote M for male. The following line asked for his address. He wrote his street number with no problem but had no room left to write the street name. Should he write it underneath the line? Did he need to start over? Because he wasn't sure, he decided to ask the librarian. Secretly he hoped that by continuing to annoy her that she would just let him check out the book. But he had no luck.

"You'll need to fill out a new form and write smaller," she ordered him, frowning.

"Can't you just use the form I filled out to get my library card? I mean, the one my mother filled out?" Luke pleaded.

"I'm afraid not. Library policy."

Once again Luke returned to the table to complete the form. He remembered to put his last name first, marked his gender, and wrote his address as small as he could. Then he saw that he had to write his birthdate and his parents' full names. He also needed to write his email address (he didn't have one) and his phone number. He wrote his phone number because that was easy and then he had an idea. He would just turn in the form, pretending it was finished, so he could check out the book and go.

"Here it is," he said cheerfully.

"Great!" the librarian said, smiling in return. "Let's see. Oh, you didn't finish it," she said, the smile fading. "You have to fill this in and this and this, see?"

"Well, I don't have an email address."

"Put your parents' email then."

"I don't know it."

"Okay, why don't you just take the form home then," she said.

"Okay. Can I check out my book and bring the form back later?"

"I'm afraid not."

Luke tried to remember that he was a member of the royal family as he smiled in a forced kind of way and took the form with him. He couldn't help but stomp all the way home, however.

His father was reading the paper in the sunroom and noticed Luke coming in. "Did you get your book, Luke?"

"No," he said, scowling.

"Why not?"

"Because I couldn't fill out the form to get a new library card."

"What? Did you tell her that none of your information had changed?"

"I asked if she could just use the old form again and she said no."

"Hm. I will need to talk with her about that. I hate unnecessary paperwork! But why couldn't you fill out the form?"

"It's so confusing and you have to write so small!" he exclaimed. "Here it is. I don't have an email address. I just wanted my book!" he said, handing the form to his father.

"I don't see any unnecessary questions here at least. But it bothers me that you have to fill out a new form when nothing has changed."

"Will you tell her to give me the book?"

"Yes, but you'll have to finish the form. I'll give you the information you need, but you need practice completing forms. They are a part of life, Luke."

When Luke sighed, his father continued, "I'm glad you brought this to my attention. I can talk with the librarian about a change of policy. But you have also reminded me that the guardians all need to know how to complete forms. We fill out forms when we apply for jobs, see a doctor, or open a bank account. I believe there is an entry on forms in the guidebook. Why don't we go read it together?"

Luke agreed and once in the castle library, read this entry aloud:

Completing Forms
To complete a form, read it over carefully before beginning to write. The directions may require it to be completed digitally or in pen, for example. Some

forms require you to make one choice, while others will ask you to check as many options as apply. Most forms have limited space, so write small for hand-written forms.

Family name means the same as *last name*. Title refers to Mr., Miss, Mrs., or Dr. Birthdates may be written as MM/DD/YY or MM/DD/YYYY where the four Y's indicate the full year rather than the last two digits of the year.

Keeping a paper or digital form with all of your important information on it will help you when you are completing new forms in the future.

"Do we have the information that I can use to complete my form on file?" Luke asked hopefully.

"Absolutely!" the king said proudly. "Screen, please pull up our reference information." When Screen produced the file, the king asked, "Do you have your form with you?"

"I do."

The king watched approvingly as Luke completed his library card application.

"Nice work, Luke! There's just one more thing you need to do."

"Get my book, I know!"

"Well, there may be two more things then. The other guardians have to know how to complete forms too. I suggest you work with Screen to create a mission for them called Forms and then you can get your book."

Luke was a little disappointed that he couldn't get his book right away. But he did agree that his fellow guardians needed to know how to complete forms.

What does *envisioned* mean?

What year were you born using just two digits?

What did Luke do wrong on his library card applications?

Chapter 32

The English children were enjoying a snack on the patio when they saw the butler come into the sunroom with the mail. Only occasionally did they receive something addressed to them. But they were always interested **nonetheless**.

★ ★ ★ ★ ★ ★ ★ ★ ★ ★
nonetheless – *even so*
★ ★ ★ ★ ★ ★ ★ ★ ★ ★

Luke was the first to get to the pile of mail sitting on the desk. When he saw a package addressed to the three of them, he motioned for his brother and sister to join him inside.

"What is it?" Ellen asked wonderingly.

"I don't know," Kirk answered. "I'm not expecting anything, are you, Luke?"

"Nope," Luke said.

Kirk retrieved a box cutter from the drawer and opened the package carefully. Luke was trying to reach into the box before Kirk had finished the job. "Luke, wait a second! I could accidentally cut you," he said irritably.

"Okay," Luke agreed, realizing he had been overly anxious to get his hands on whatever was inside.

When Kirk finished opening the box, he withdrew a headset of some sort, wrapped in plastic.

It was Luke's turn to ask what it was.

"I'm not sure," Kirk answered, slowly removing the plastic wrap.

Luke grabbed it hastily when Kirk had finished and put it on. "Cool!" he cried.

"Luke, I was looking at that!" Kirk objected.

Luke reached into the box and pulled out another identical headset wrapped in plastic. "Here's another one for you," he said, handing it to Kirk. "And hey! There's one for you too, Ellen," he said passing the headset to his sister.

Ellen unwrapped hers and asked her brothers what it was for.

"I don't know, but they obviously work with this," Kirk said, taking a black rectangular device from the box. "Oh good," he continued. "There are directions." He pulled a white booklet from the bottom of the package.

The three of them tried to read the booklet together to determine what the device was for. "It's a gaming device," Kirk said.

"Wow! Kirk, I think it's holographic!" Luke shrieked excitedly.

"What do you mean, holographic?" Ellen asked.

"Holographic means that you are **immersed** in the gaming world. You can see the characters and the landscape just like you are in the game," Kirk explained.

★ ★ ★ ★ ★ ★ ★ ★ ★ ★

immersed – *engrossed*

★ ★ ★ ★ ★ ★ ★ ★ ★ ★

"That's amazing!"

"Let's go to the game room and try it out!" Luke urged them. Neither sibling had anything planned for the afternoon. And truthfully, they were just as eager as Luke to try it. They spent the rest of the day setting up the game and learning how to use it.

At dinner that evening, they chatted excitedly about the game they had received.

"Did you order this for them, dear?" the king asked the queen.

"No, but I wish I had because they love it so much," the queen replied.

The conversation turned to the delicious meal that was served to them.

The English children spent time playing with their new game system every day that week. Luke even tried putting the headset on Comet, but he would shake it off before he was able to see the game in action. The three of them were in the game room when the king joined them, looking distressed.

"What is it, Father?" Kirk was first to ask.

"Who sent you this game system?" he asked.

"Uh, I'm not sure. What's the name of the company, Luke?" Kirk asked.

"I don't remember," Luke said, continuing to play the game.

"Luke, turn the game off," the king said sternly.

"What's wrong, Father?" Ellen asked.

"What's wrong is that the company who sent you this game— Happy Holographics—is very *un*happy. They complained on Social Universe that despite sending you their latest and greatest game system as a gift, they have not received a thank you."

"Oh," Ellen said, staring at the floor with a guilty expression.

"Did you post on Social Universe—I mean, did you have your virtual assistant post on Social Universe that we love it? Because we do!" Luke said.

"No, Luke. I'm sure Happy Holographics would love to have your review of their system posted on Social Universe. But what they really want is a written thank-you note," the king explained.

"What kind of thank-you note?" Kirk asked.

"The usual. The kind you send when you get a gift." When he noticed his children's blank expressions, he asked, "You've sent thank-you notes, right?"

The three English children slowly shook their heads no.

"What?" The king was aghast. "Why not?"

Ellen was the first to speak. "We don't really know how. We have said thank you, of course. We have even said thanks with our communicators, but we have never written a thank-you note. I have heard of them, though."

The king sighed heavily. "There may come a day when people don't send written thank-you notes. But they are still considered good

165

manners. The people at Happy Holographics aren't the only ones who will be unhappy if they don't receive one from you in the future."

"We're sorry for not sending a thank-you note, Father. How do we do it?" Ellen asked.

"First, you need a card or stationery. I know we have some thank-you notes around here somewhere." The king contacted his assistant who brought some thank-you notes to the game room.

Ellen thought they were beautiful. "If we had some blank cards, could we make our own thank-you notes?"

"Indeed! That would be very nice," the king agreed. "Now then, you open the card and write your thank-you note."

"With a pencil?" Luke asked.

"Thank-you notes are normally written in ink. But beginning writers like you can write them in pencil so mistakes can be erased."

Luke was pleased with his father's answer. He got some writing instruments for himself and his siblings from the game cabinet.

"And you start with…?" Kirk asked when he had a pen in hand.

"Dear Happy Holographics team," the king answered.

"Uh, can you spell Holographics?" Luke asked.

After the king helped Luke with his spelling, the three children asked what came next. "Well, you thank them," the king replied, looking uncomfortable.

Ellen frowned. "So just say thank you?"

"No." The king groaned. "I need your mother." He contacted her via communicator and asked her to join them in the game room.

When she arrived, the king explained that he wasn't sure what to write in a thank-you note. "Oh, thank-you notes can be so encouraging if they're written well," she gushed. "What is the thank-you for?"

The children explained that they were thanking the company for sending them the holographic game.

"My word! I should say you should send them a thank-you note," she exclaimed. "Such a generous gift."

"Mother, what should we write?" Ellen asked.

"Of course you will write 'Thank you for the game.' But what makes a thank-you note truly exceptional is writing something more."

"Like what?" Kirk asked.

"Like that you've been playing it nonstop since it arrived! Or that you love surprises or that all their hard work paid off because their game is amazing. You make them feel like the gift matters to you."

"I feel really bad that I haven't thanked them before," Ellen said sadly.

"Me too," Luke sighed.

"Well, why don't you write that? I'm sure you can make up for any hard feelings."

The queen inspired them to write and when they were finished, she added, "Be sure to sign it. When you are writing to a friend or family member, it is customary to use the closing 'Love.' However, 'Sincerely' or 'With gratitude' would be lovely for this occasion."

When they were finished, the queen had them address the envelope. They asked Screen to provide them with the company address. An assistant took them to be mailed.

"I feel so much better," Ellen said.

"Me too," Luke agreed.

"I don't," Kirk said. In response to the **quizzical** looks he received, he explained, "If we don't know how to write thank-you notes, my guess is the other guardians don't either. I think we need to send out a mission on thank-you notes."

★ ★ ★ ★ ★ ★ ★ ★ ★ ★

quizzical – *questioning*

★ ★ ★ ★ ★ ★ ★ ★ ★ ★

"That's a great idea, Kirk!" Ellen said.

The three of them created a mission for the guardians, asking their mother for advice as they worked.

What does *quizzical* mean?

Why was Happy Holographics unhappy?

Why isn't it enough to just write 'thank you' in a note?

167

Chapter 33

Giggles were **emanating** from the castle kitchen. Ellen and her mother were inside making ice cream cone cupcakes for Luke's birthday. Cook was watching but had been **forbidden** to help as the two royal ladies wanted to do it themselves.

"This is so much fun," the queen gushed. "And aren't these aprons gorgeous?"

"Yes! I love them," Ellen agreed.

"Okay, so first we are supposed to make the cake mix as directed on the box. What does it say we need?"

"It says to add a stick of butter to the cake mix." Ellen eagerly removed the wrapper from the stick of butter and added it to the bowl with the mix. She grabbed a large spoon and started to stir. "Hm. This isn't easy. Mother, can you try?"

The queen began stirring vigorously but was also having difficulty. Cook bit her lip to keep from saying anything. Finally the queen said, "What else do the directions say?"

Ellen read from the back of the cake mix box. "It says to soften the butter."

"Soften the butter? I guess that means to heat it?" the queen said, glancing at Cook for approval. "We should put it in the microwave then I suppose." The queen was about to put the entire metal bowl into the microwave when Cook stopped her. Without a word, she removed the majority of the butter and put it in a glass bowl. She handed it to the queen with a smile.

"Very well then," the queen said, gratefully putting the bowl in the microwave. And I suppose I should set it for...?"

Cook set the timer on the microwave without speaking. The queen removed the bowl when the timer went off. She added the now softened butter to the large bowl with the cake mix. "Okay, we are all set now!" she declared.

"We have to add water and three whole eggs," Ellen read from the box. Ellen carefully measured the water and added it to the mix. Cook handed her a carton of eggs from the refrigerator. Ellen gleefully removed three eggs from the carton and gently placed them in the bowl.

She was about to resume stirring when Cook laughed out loud. Without saying a word, she removed the eggs from Ellen's bowl and cracked them into a smaller bowl. She handed the smaller bowl to Ellen and urged her to continue. "Ohhhh," she said, embarrassed.

Ellen and the cook took turns stirring the batter by hand until it was smooth. Cook decided it was too risky to let them use a mixer. The queen said, "The recipe says we are to pour the batter into muffin tins." Cook quickly produced the tins and the queen carefully poured the batter into the individual openings. "No spills!" she declared proudly. "Now what?"

Ellen looked at the recipe on her mother's tablet. "Now we add paper baking cups." Both ladies looked to Cook, who was shaking her head.

"What is it?" the queen asked her.

"You can't add paper cups after you've put the batter in the tin."

"Oh dear. What do we do?"

"Thankfully, these are nonstick pans, so you don't have to have them."

"Oh good," the queen said with relief. Truth be told, she had no idea what paper baking cups were, but she was glad she didn't need them. "What's next then, Ellen?"

"We preheat the oven to 325 degrees Fahrenheit for our nonstick pan." Ellen was proud that she had made note of the kind of pan they were using.

Cook couldn't stand saying silent any longer. "Preheating the oven is the first thing you're supposed to do. You don't do it after you pour the batter into the tin."

"That's odd," the queen said. "Look at the recipe, Cook. We're following it in order."

Cook picked up the tablet and clucked disapprovingly. "This recipe is completely out of order."

The queen was near tears. "Oh no. This won't do. We wanted to do something special for Luke's birthday!"

"No worries, Your Majesty," Cook comforted her. "We can fix this recipe right up and Luke will love it!"

The three ladies worked together to add the ice cream cones to the cakes before baking them.

Kirk was in the computer lab where he was also preparing a surprise for Luke's birthday. He was trying to program a robot to put Luke's dirty clothes in his hamper. He had found the directions online. Despite following them carefully, the robot wasn't working.

When he found himself getting very frustrated, he had an idea. He would speak to the new head programmer. He contacted him via communicator and explained what he was trying to do. Soon he joined Kirk in the lab.

"I don't know what I'm doing wrong," Kirk explained.

"Can I see the directions you're using?" the programmer asked.

Kirk opened the screen with the directions and the programmer looked them over. "I know what your problem is, Kirk."

"You do?"

"Yes, these directions are out of order."

"Ugh! I wasted all this time! Well, thank you so much for your help."

"No problem. What are you going to do now?"

"I guess I'll try to find new directions that will actually work."

"Do you want me to check them over before you start working with them?" the programmer offered.

"That would actually be great," Kirk said.

Kirk watched as the programmer reviewed a second set of instructions and frowned. "Kirk, these are all out of order too. You'll give yourself a headache trying to use these. I tell you what. I can help you program the robot for Luke."

"That is so nice of you! I will take you up on your offer."

The two were still programming when Ellen burst into the room. "Kirk, Mother and I made the most amazing dessert for Luke's birthday! Oh, sorry. I didn't know you had company."

Kirk looked apologetically at the programmer. "It's okay. We're working on a gift for Luke too." Kirk explained his idea and described the problem they had with the directions being out of order.

"That's strange. Our recipe was out of order too," Ellen said.

"Uh-oh. You don't suppose all the directions in the galaxy are mixed up? What a mess that would be!" Kirk said. He excused himself from the room after making sure the programmer was alright with continuing to work on the coding himself. "You better come with me, Ellen."

The two went to the castle library. "There have to be some 'How To' books in here," Kirk said, pulling his finger along a shelf of books. "Ah, here we are. *How To Take Care of Your Teeth.* Let's see," he said, scanning the pages. "First, turn on the water. Second, spit into the sink and rinse it down the drain. Third, use a toothbrush to carefully brush each surface of your teeth in a circular motion. Finally, add a small strip of toothpaste to the brush."

"Uh, yeah, that's not right," Ellen giggled.

"No," Kirk sighed. "We have a big problem. Screen," he called out. "Is there anything going on in the galaxy that has to do with directions?"

Images of various locations in the galaxy scrolled across the screen. "This is the only news I have, Your Highness." A video began playing. A siren blared while sentences ran from a building called Direction Towers. They waited outside.

"What's going on there?" Kirk asked.

"**Mandatory** fire drills," Screen replied.

★ ★ ★ ★ ★ ★ ★ ★ ★ ★

mandatory – *required*

★ ★ ★ ★ ★ ★ ★ ★ ★ ★

The two watched as the siren stopped and the sentences began returning to the building. A camera followed them in and witnessed the confusion as they tried to return to the floor they came from.

"I think I know why our directions are all mixed up. I'm going to have to get Father to stop the fire drills in Direction Towers. That's causing the problem," Kirk said.

"But what do we do about the directions that are already mixed up?" Ellen asked.

Kirk smiled. "I have an idea."

The two of them wrote a mission for the guardians called "Directions." Kirk then returned to the computer lab. He hoped he could help the programmer finish his robot surprise for Luke.

What does *mandatory* mean?

What was wrong with the tooth brushing directions?

Why were all the directions mixed up?

Chapter 34

Ellen urged her mother to walk faster. She was on her way to her first meeting of Grammar Girls and she couldn't have been more excited. "Did you just love Grammar Girls when you were my age, Mother?" she asked.

"Oh yes! We had so much fun," the queen answered. She was a little breathless from trying to keep up with her daughter.

"What were your favorite activities?"

The queen slowed down a bit to think. "I think it was writing stories together. We would each take turns writing a line and we would laugh so hard at the crazy results."

"That sounds like so much fun!" Ellen said. "Let's hurry and get there." The queen laughed at Ellen's eagerness.

When the two arrived at the meeting, the group leader introduced herself and welcomed them. She explained that the queen didn't have to stay but could pick Ellen up at the end of the meeting. The queen kissed Ellen good-bye and told her to have fun. That's exactly what Ellen planned on doing.

The first girls she met seemed really nice and the snacks that were sitting out looked delectable. When the leader was sure all the girls had arrived, she called them to sit in a circle together. "Welcome to Grammar Girls! I'm your leader, Mrs. G. I have two daughters—one grown and one in this troop," she said. She exchanged smiles with her daughter. "I love to bake, so I've made some of my favorite cookies for us to enjoy later. But what I really love to do is write! We're going to do a lot of writing in this group."

The girls smiled and whispered excitedly to one another. "Now then," Mrs. G. continued. "We will start by introducing ourselves." She turned to Ellen on her right. "Why don't you go first?"

Ellen's smile faded and she felt sick. She stared at the girls and opened her mouth and closed it. She stared at the floor. She willed herself to say something, but nothing happened. As the awkward silence dragged on, the other girls looked at one another. They wondered what was wrong. Ellen turned her terrified eyes to the leader and wordlessly pleaded for help. "Okay, you can introduce yourself later," Mrs. G. said reassuringly. "Why don't you start?" she asked the girl to the right of Ellen.

Ellen didn't hear much of what the other girls said. *What is wrong with me?* she asked herself. *Why didn't I just introduce myself?*

★ ★ ★ ★ ★ ★ ★ ★ ★ ★

When the introductions were over, the girls played some fun grammar games. Ellen noticed that the other girls seemed **wary** around her. Even though she had been looking forward to Mrs. G's cookies, she found that she had lost her appetite.

★ ★ ★ ★ ★ ★ ★ ★ ★ ★

wary – *cautious*
appalling – *awful*

★ ★ ★ ★ ★ ★ ★ ★ ★ ★

The queen arrived to pick up Ellen and Ellen rushed to her. Mrs. G. told the queen it was lovely to have Ellen, but the queen picked up from her tone of voice that something was wrong.

As Ellen and her mother walked back to the castle, Ellen burst into tears. "Oh my!" the queen cried. "I was going to ask how it went, but I already know."

"Oh, Mother, it was **appalling**!" Ellen sobbed.

"My word! What was so bad? Mrs. G. seems so nice."

"She is," Ellen said, inhaling loudly, before crying some more.

"Was it the other girls then?"

174

"No," Ellen said, squeezing her eyes shut and sobbing silently. "It—was—me," she croaked.

"You? You're a lovely young lady. What's wrong with you?"

"I—couldn't—," Ellen stammered, covering her face with her hands.

"You couldn't what?"

"I couldn't introduce myself!" Ellen wailed.

"Ohhh," the queen said, finally understanding.

"It was horrible! They all think I'm weird now," Ellen said, using the tissue her mother handed her to dry her tears.

"Oh, I doubt they think you're weird."

"No, they do! I would think I was weird," Ellen insisted.

"Come on. Let's go home and talk about this."

Ellen reluctantly accompanied her mother home. She begged to be allowed to take a nap before dinner. The queen agreed, thinking some rest would make her daughter feel better.

At dinner that evening, Ellen looked fresher and the queen was relieved. "How was Grammar Girls?" the king asked, much to the queen's **chagrin**.

★ ★ ★ ★ ★ ★ ★ ★ ★ ★

chagrin – *irritation*

★ ★ ★ ★ ★ ★ ★ ★ ★ ★

"Uh, it was fine, dear," the queen answered him. She raised her eyebrows to communicate that he should drop the subject. The king missed the signal.

"So you liked it?" he asked.

Ellen groaned. "I made a fool of myself actually."

"What? I don't believe it," the king argued.

"Well, I did. I couldn't introduce myself to the group. I just kept staring, unable to speak. I'm sure the other girls think I'm weird now," Ellen said in frustration.

"I see," the king said, suddenly taking a serious tone. "I think I know what the problem is."

"You do?" Ellen's face brightened. "Could this be the Gremlin's doing? I didn't even think of that!"

"Were the other girls able to introduce themselves?" he asked.

"Yes. Are you saying that it's not the Gremlin then? Ugh. It's official. I am a weirdo," Ellen groaned.

"Ellen," the king said sternly. "Stage fright is the most common fear in the galaxy. It hardly makes you a weirdo. I don't want you to speak negatively about yourself."

"What do you mean 'stage fright'? I wasn't on a stage. We were just sitting in a circle."

"Stage fright means that you are nervous speaking or performing in front of people. Were you nervous about introducing yourself?"

"Yes," Ellen admitted. "But I shouldn't have been! The other girls didn't seem to be."

"The other girls probably were nervous, Ellen," her mother added. "I was nervous my first time in Grammar Girls."

"You were?" Ellen asked in surprise.

"Oh yes."

"But did you just keep staring and not talking like I did? Ugh! It was so embarrassing," Ellen complained.

"No, but I had had practice introducing myself," the queen explained. "I learned that I should smile, look people in the eye, and share something that makes me unique."

"Have we had the children practice introducing themselves?" the king asked.

This time the queen looked embarrassed. "I may have forgotten to have them practice. Oh dear. It's really my fault you had such a hard time. Please forgive me, will you, Ellen?"

"Of course, Mother. But can we practice right after dinner?" she asked eagerly.

"Absolutely! We will practice enough that the next time you go to Grammar Girls you will be a pro at introducing yourself."

For the first time since the meeting, Ellen seemed happy.

"Wonderful!" the king declared. "Now let's eat." The rest of the family had to laugh.

"Father?" Luke asked. "Do you think I should practice with them? I'll be old enough for Grammar Guys soon. I don't want to have that stage fright thing. It sounds awful!"

The king chuckled. "Luke, you should definitely practice with them. In fact, now that I think of it, I want all the guardians to practice introducing themselves. After your mother helps you, will you create a mission?"

The three children agreed and started eating. Ellen's appetite had returned.

What does *appalling* mean?

What is stage fright?

How should you introduce yourself?

Chapter 35

The royal family was enjoying a light lunch out on the patio when the conversation turned to the Poetry Reading Festival that was beginning that evening.

"Do you know what you're reading, Luke? I do," Ellen said.

"Of course I do. 'My Shadow' by Robert Louis Stevenson," he replied.

"Oh, that's a good one. I have mine memorized. How about you?"

"We don't have to have it memorized, do we, Mother?" Luke asked.

"No, you don't. It is a poetry *reading* festival after all," the queen said, smiling. Luke grinned victoriously at his sister. The queen noted Luke's reaction and continued. "However, it is a good idea to be very familiar with the poetry you are reading." It was Ellen's turn to feel victorious. Luke shrugged and focused on his sandwich.

"Kirk, are you going to be reading a poem you wrote?" the queen asked.

"I am."

"Wonderful!" she exclaimed.

"We are really looking forward to hearing you children read," the king said, polishing off his sandwich.

"We are indeed," the queen said.

Kirk and Ellen used the rest of the afternoon to practice, but Luke and Comet spent their time in the game room. Happy Holographics had sent the children their latest game and Luke couldn't resist playing it. The thank-you note had already been sent, so he didn't see a reason not to play. He planned to practice his poetry reading the last hour before dinner time. He figured there would be plenty of practice time.

However, he was startled when he received a reminder on his communicator that dinner was being served. Because they were leaving immediately afterward for the festival, it left him no time to practice. Luke consoled himself with the fact that he had read the

178

poem once when he was choosing what to read. It wasn't like he had to have it memorized. His mother had said so!

After dinner, Luke didn't fuss about his appearance the way his mother and sister did. The poetry festival wasn't a formal occasion, so Luke was allowed to dress casually. He was glad.

They traveled in the royal spacecopter, which Luke loved. They arrived at the amphitheater in plenty of time. The queen had made sure of that. "It's so exciting, isn't it?" she asked the children, when they found their seats. "This is one of my favorite events."

"Mine too," Ellen agreed.

Before long, the emcee took the stage and welcomed everyone to thunderous applause. "The Annual Poetry Reading Festival keeps the art form of poetry alive in the galaxy. Poetry teaches children how to read, write, and understand what they read. It encourages emotional expression and **empathetic** listening. We are proud of the students who have volunteered this year. They will either read poetry aloud or share their own poetry. Could I ask the readers to make their way to the seats behind me? Let's show them our appreciation as they do!"

★ ★ ★ ★ ★ ★ ★ ★ ★ ★

empathetic – *sympathetic*

anonymous – *unknown*

★ ★ ★ ★ ★ ★ ★ ★ ★ ★

The three English children said their good-byes to their parents and made their way to the stage while the crowd applauded.

"We'll begin with our youngest readers," the emcee continued. "They're always a crowd favorite." He introduced a little girl whose pigtails bobbed as she approached the microphone. The emcee made a show of adjusting it low enough so she could speak into it. She read:

"Days of the Month" – Author, **Anonymous**

Thirty days hath September,
April, June, and November;
February has twenty-eight alone.
All the rest have thirty-one,
Excepting leap-year—that's the time
When February's days are twenty-nine.

She curtsied when she was done and the crowd roared their approval. The emcee was still applauding when he returned to the microphone. "Wasn't that fabulous?" He introduced two more readers who were also well received. Then the emcee introduced Luke.

Luke looked to Ellen and Kirk for encouragement before he stood up. They nodded at him and he made his way to the microphone, poem in hand. He noticed that the paper was trembling in his hand and that the print suddenly seemed very small.

"'My Shadow' by Robert Louis Stevenson," he read. He looked up at the crowd nervously and quickly returned his focus to the paper in front of him. "I have a—, a little shadow that goes in—, and out with, with me," he stammered. He looked up to see if he could see his parents' reaction. When he looked back at the paper, he couldn't find where he had left off. "Uh, sorry," he said. "Here it is. 'And what can be the use, the use?— of him is, is more than I can, than I can see'," he continued haltingly.

Luke sighed, realizing that he should have practiced. He struggled through the rest of the poem and seemed ashamed by the applause. He returned to his seat, looking very **dejected**.

★ ★ ★ ★ ★ ★ ★ ★ ★ ★

dejected – *sad*

★ ★ ★ ★ ★ ★ ★ ★ ★ ★

His disappointment in himself grew when he heard Ellen and Kirk do an excellent job reading their poetry. He couldn't wait for the event to be over, but when it was, he dreaded facing his parents. He decided he would apologize for embarrassing them before they could say anything.

His mother hugged him and told him, "You did not embarrass us, Luke. We love you. It takes courage to read in front of people like that. Not everyone volunteers!"

"That's right, son," the king said, patting him on the back.

"I should have practiced! I failed!" Luke wailed. "Kirk and Ellen were so good."

"If you learned the value of practice, it isn't a failure at all. It's a lesson learned," the king replied.

Kirk and Ellen agreed with their father and told Luke to cheer up. They were going to experience one of their favorite parts of the Poetry Reading Festival tradition: going out for ice cream!

At the ice cream shop, the family continued discussing the poetry readings. Kirk and Ellen debated their favorite poems of the night. The king and queen agreed that some of the original poetry, including Kirk's, had been excellent. But Luke couldn't get past his own struggle on stage.

"It's true I didn't practice, but I still don't think I would have been as good as Kirk or Ellen if I had," he moaned.

"Do you really want to get better at reading poetry?" the king asked him.

"Yes!"

"Good, because reading aloud is a very important skill. Just like introductions, it is something we are often asked to do," the king responded.

"Can you tell me how to improve?"

"I can do better than that, Luke. The guidebook has a section on reading aloud. You may find it under reading fluency. In fact, now that I think about it, this is something every guardian needs to know. After you look it up, I would like the three of you to send out a mission."

The three of them gladly agreed. Even Kirk and Ellen found the guidebook information on reading fluency helpful.

Reading Fluency

Reading fluency or smoothness requires knowledge of phonics and vocabulary. Before reading aloud, make sure you know all the words and how they should be pronounced or spoken. Practice, practice, practice to improve speed. With time, you can be saying one word and reading the next few or noticing upcoming punctuation. Reading skills improve by imitating another reader.

Some reading aloud tips include:

1. Emphasize or stress the words that rhyme in poetry.

2. Look up from a reading to make eye contact occasionally. Hold your finger at the place you last read so you won't lose your place.

3. Use different voices for characters in a children's book.

4. Change your loudness or speed every so often to keep listeners' attention.

5. Drop your tone when coming to a period to signal the end of a sentence.

What does *anonymous* mean?

Why didn't Luke practice his poetry reading?

How could he have done a better job?

Chapter 36

"Luke, I'm so proud of how hard you've been working on reading aloud," the king told him at breakfast one morning.

Luke was thrilled. "Thank you, Father. It's actually fun!"

"I'm so glad you said that. The main library branch is starting a storytelling hour. I told the librarians in charge that you'd be glad to volunteer."

"To read stories?"

"Well, I think so, yes," the king agreed.

"So I would just go and read books to younger kids?"

"I think so. You will have to get the details when you meet with library staff today."

"Today?" Luke asked.

"Yes. Why wait? I know they want to have their first storytelling hour next week and you love to read stories. You can talk with them about what the requirements are and the schedule. Okay?"

"Sure, I guess so."

Luke felt a little nervous as he walked to the library that afternoon. He was really getting better at reading aloud, but he wasn't sure he was **qualified** to lead a story hour. He decided that he would be honest with them and they could decide if they still wanted him.

★ ★ ★ ★ ★ ★ ★ ★ ★ ★

qualified – *able*

flattered – *praised*

★ ★ ★ ★ ★ ★ ★ ★ ★ ★

When he arrived, he asked to meet with the two women whose names his father had given him. In a few minutes they greeted him warmly and asked him to join them in a meeting room to talk.

"We understand you are really a good storyteller," one of them **flattered** him.

"Well, I don't know—"

"Your father tells us it's become your new hobby," the other librarian interjected.

"I do like to—"

"That's wonderful! We have been wanting to offer a storytelling hour for ages. It sounds like you'll be a perfect fit," the first librarian said. She turned to the other woman who was nodding vigorously.

"I uh—what would I be doing exactly?" Luke asked.

"What you do best. Telling stories!" the second librarian exclaimed, patting him on the arm.

"Will you pick out the books I'll be reading or do you want me to choose them?"

The librarians looked confused. "Oh no. You won't be reading from books. You'll be telling us the stories," the first one said.

"Telling us the stories? I'm not sure what you mean."

"You know, the stories that you've been working on. We can't wait to hear them!" the second librarian gushed.

"I think there has been a mistake. I don't tell stories. I read stories aloud. I've really been having fun creating voices for characters," he explained, regaining his pride a little.

"Oh...well, I think this will work out well," the second librarian said.

"You do?" Luke asked hopefully.

"Yes," she continued. "Storytelling isn't much different than reading aloud. We'd love to have you!" The first librarian nodded her agreement.

"Well, I—"

"It's settled then!" the first librarian exclaimed. "We will see you next Saturday at 10 a.m. We really can't wait!"

"We can't!" the second librarian agreed.

"Okay, but—"

"We'll see you out, Luke. Thanks so much for coming in and being willing to share your talent with us," the first librarian said. She opened the meeting room door and showed him out.

As Luke walked home, he wondered what had just happened. Somehow he had agreed to tell stories at the library when he didn't know the first thing about telling stories! He started to panic until he decided on a plan. He would have his father call them and explain things to them. After all, he had gotten him into this mess.

He found his father in the study, eager to hear how the meeting had gone.

"It didn't go well, Father," he said.

"You mean they didn't want you? My goodness. Did you read for them? If not, why don't you go back and insist on showing them how well you read?"

"No, no, that's not it."

"So they do want you?"

"Yes—"

"That's excellent! I knew they would recognize talent when they saw it. I'm proud of you, Luke."

"Thank you, Father, but—"

"Luke, listen, I want to hear all about your meeting at dinner, but I am expecting a call about the comma conflict. My word, people get so upset about comma usage! I will see you later," the king said, opening the door for Luke.

★ ★ ★ ★ ★ ★ ★ ★ ★ ★

dumbfounded – *stunned*

★ ★ ★ ★ ★ ★ ★ ★ ★ ★

Luke was **dumbfounded**. What was he supposed to do now? He was also frustrated but knew better than to interrupt his father during an important call. He decided to talk to Comet about it until he could have his father's full attention.

At dinner that evening, the king raised the subject first. "I am so proud of our boy, dear. He is officially a library storyteller!"

The rest of the family clapped and congratulated him.

"Ugh!" he exclaimed. When he noted his family members' surprise, he rushed to explain.

"Let me tell you what happened. First, Father told the librarians that I was a great storyteller and set up a meeting. So I went to the meeting today, thinking that I could just tell them that I really like to read stories and they could tell me if that was what they wanted.

"But I got to the library and they wouldn't even let me talk! They just kept telling me how they had heard what a great storyteller I was and that they were so thrilled to have me. When I asked them if they would be picking out the books or I would be, they were so confused. They said, 'Oh no! You will be telling your own stories!' And I thought, what? I don't tell my own stories!

"Even after I explained that, they told me that I could tell my own stories just as easily as reading stories. They said they would see me on Saturday morning and almost shoved me out the door! So then I was freaking out. I'm thinking, I'm supposed to tell stories to a bunch of little kids and I don't even have any stories and what am I supposed to do? So then I thought, I'll just have Father call them and explain the whole thing and get me out of it.

"But when I tried to talk to you about it, Father, you just said you were glad they saw my talent. You couldn't talk to me because you had an important call. So now I'm still supposed to tell stories and I just can't!" Luke sat dejected with his head in his hands when he was done.

"Luke, I know you're upset, but please don't put your elbows on the table," the queen corrected him. Luke removed his elbows and looked so upset that his mother got up to hug him. "Luke, everything is going to be okay."

"Indeed it will be," the king agreed.

"You'll tell them I can't do it then?" Luke asked with renewed hope.

"Oh no. I'm going to tell them that you're an incredible storyteller!" The rest of the family gasped.

"Before you say anything," the king continued, "let me explain. What you did just now was storytelling. Didn't he have our attention as he was telling us what happened today?" he asked, looking at the rest of the family. They nodded, beginning to understand the king's point.

"So I'm supposed to tell the kids stories about what happened to me?" Luke asked, still confused.

"You could. But storytelling also means telling stories you've read, but without the book. You have the dramatic part down!" he exclaimed.

"I still don't understand."

The king requested that the guidebook be brought to the dining room. When it arrived, he read the section on storytelling aloud.

Storytelling

Storytelling has been practiced for thousands of years. It is useful for teaching, motivating, and entertaining. Everyone tells stories, but to improve your storytelling skills, follow these steps:

Choose a story. To begin, choose a short story that you love. It could be a personal story or a story you've read. Stories that have repetitive parts are great choices. *The Three Little Pigs*'s "Then I'll huff and I'll puff and I'll blow your house in!" is an example.

Memorize the story. Make notes or use pictures of the main parts of the story and use them to tell the story after you've practiced. Keep telling the story until you can do it without notes.

Bring the story to life. Use your voice and your movements to create characters and act the story out. Use a prop or object if it adds to the story. Get your audience involved. Look them in the eye. Ask them to add the sounds to the story (like knocking) or say repeated dialogue (like "Not by the hair of my chinny-chin-chin!").

> **Try it out**. When you have your story ready, perform it for your family members or friends. Did you lose their interest at any point? What could you do to keep them involved in the story?
>
> Keep telling stories and you will improve your storytelling skills.

"Well, Luke, what do you think?" the king asked.

Luke grinned. "I think it actually sounds like fun." The rest of the family applauded him again.

"We can't wait to hear your first story, Luke," his father said.

"There's just one thing," Luke said. When his family waited for him to continue, he explained. "I think the other guardians should know how to tell stories too."

The king smiled. "I was hoping you would say that. Why don't you three kids put a storytelling mission together?" Kirk, Luke, and Ellen got busy doing just that when they finished dinner.

What does *flattered* mean?

What problem was Luke having that needed to be solved?

What is one way to become a better storyteller?

About the Author

Dr. Melanie Wilson was a clinical psychologist working in a Christian practice, a college instructor, freelance writer, and public speaker before she felt called to stay home and educate her children. She is a mother of six and has homeschooled for 16 years. She says it's her most fulfilling vocation.

Melanie has always been passionate about language arts and used bits and pieces of different curriculum and approaches to teach her children and friends' children. In 2014, she believed she had another calling to write the curriculum she had always wanted as a homeschooling mom — one that didn't take a lot of time, made concepts simple and memorable, and was enough fun to keep her kids motivated.

Books have been a family business since the beginning. Melanie's husband Mark has been selling library books for 30 years. Melanie and the older kids frequently pitch in to help at the annual librarians' conference. Grammar Galaxy is another family business that she hopes will be a great learning opportunity for their children.

When Melanie isn't busy homeschooling, visiting her oldest son in college, or writing, she loves to play tennis with family and friends.

Melanie is also the author of *The Organized Homeschool Life* and *So You're Not Wonder Woman*. Learn more on her blog, Psychowith6.com.

About the Illustrator

Rebecca Mueller has had an interest in drawing from an early age. Rebecca quickly developed a unique style and illustrated her first books, a short series of bedtime stories with her mother, at age 9. She has since illustrated for other authors and does graphic design work for several organizations. Rebecca is currently studying at the Pierre Laclede Honors College at the University of Missouri - St. Louis and is working towards a BA in English with a minor in Studio Art - Graphic Design.

Made in the USA
Monee, IL
16 June 2024